# How To Run And Grow
# Your Own Business

Kevin Duncan

Kevin Duncan worked in advertising and direct marketing for 20 years. For the past 15 years he has worked on his own as a business adviser, marketing expert and author. He advises various businesses as a non-executive director, business strategist and trainer.

His books have sold more than 120,000 copies and been translated into over a dozen languages. Several have been voted Telegraph Business Club Book of the Week, WHSmith Book of the Month, Foyles Book of the Month, and nominated for CMI Management Book of the Year.

In his spare time he travels to strange parts of the world, releases rock and blues albums, and flies birds of prey.

Also by Kevin Duncan:

*Business Greatest Hits*

*Marketing Greatest Hits*

*Marketing Greatest Hits Volume 2*

*Revolution*

*Run Your Own Business*

*Small Business Survival*

*So What?*

*Start*

*The Diagrams Book*

*The Dictionary of Business Bullshit*

*The Ideas Book*

*The Smart Thinking Book*

*Tick Achieve*

*What You Need To Know About Starting A Business*

kevinduncanexpertadvice@gmail.com

www.expertadviceonline.com

Teach<sup>®</sup> Yourself

# How To Run And Grow Your Own Business

## 20 ways to manage your business brilliantly

Kevin Duncan

First published in Great Britain in 2016 by Hodder and Stoughton. An Hachette UK company.

This edition published in 2016 by John Murray Learning

*British Library Cataloguing in Publication Data*: a catalogue record for this title is available from the British Library.

ISBN 9781473638136

eISBN 9781473638143

2

Typeset by Cenveo® Publisher Services.

Printed and bound in Great Britain by CPI Group (UK) Ltd., Croydon, CR0 4YY.

John Murray Learning policy is to use papers that are natural, renewable and recyclable products and made from wood grown in sustainable forests. The logging and manufacturing processes are expected to conform to the environmental regulations of the country of origin.

Carmelite House
50 Victoria Embankment
London EC4Y 0DZ
www.hodder.co.uk

Also available in ebook

# Contents

# Part One

## Starting and Running Your Business

# 1

# Where do I start?

In this chapter you will learn:

▶ *How to be honest with yourself*
▶ *What you need to prepare in order to be a success*
▶ *How to write a simple, realistic plan*
▶ *How to work out the materials that you need*
▶ *How to get it all under way*

It's a daunting prospect, isn't it? An empty desk, no customers, no confirmed money coming in, and no one to gossip with. Welcome to running your own business. Every issue is now yours to wrestle with, and yours alone. But then so is all the satisfaction when things go well, whether that is mental or financial. So let's dive straight in and work out how you are going to turn what many would regard as an ordeal into a fantastic success.

## Assume that you have something to offer

Let's start by assuming that there is a market for your talents, otherwise you wouldn't have got this far. We have to believe that this is true otherwise you probably wouldn't be reading this book. By now you will have established the basics in your mind. Your thought pattern will have been something along the lines of:

▶ I am good at what I do.

▶ There is a market for my product/service (whether this is actually true and how you set about proving it to yourself will come later).

▶ I can do it better on my own than in my current set-up.

▶ I have a way of doing it that people will like.

▶ What I put in and what I get out will be a better balanced equation than my current state of affairs.

That should just about cover it. Thousands of people go through this basic thought process at some point in their working lives – sometimes on many occasions. However, even if you have been able to tick all the boxes so far, the issue that you have to grapple with next is far more fundamental:

*'If I ran my own business, I'm not sure if I could live with myself.'*

What do people mean when they say this? Well, first, there are important issues with regard to exactly where you are going to do your work. What are your domestic arrangements? Could they possibly accommodate you achieving everything that you need to without disrupting all the other aspects of your life?

Second, there is your frame of mind: are you cut out to operate outside of a conventional work environment? Could you cope without the interaction? Could you motivate yourself when no one is there to give you a kick-start?

Evidence suggests that the majority of people are very capable of working on their own. They simply need a little guidance and encouragement to point them in the right direction. If you don't make the leap, you'll never know, so let's make a start.

It is essential that you feel good about yourself. You must genuinely believe that you can offer something of value to others, otherwise you would not have taken the plunge to set up on your own, or even be toying with the idea. Make this vital assumption and start from there. Don't be apologetic about your skills, either to yourself or to a potential customer. State them clearly, get used to saying them out loud, and become comfortable with explaining them to others. Without being arrogant, everyone who works on their own has to have a certain level of self-confidence. You no longer have colleagues to witness your performance and help you with encouraging observations. You rarely get debriefed objectively on how something has gone. Consequently, you have to be very adept at self-assessment. Now all the motivation has to come from within.

## Be honest with yourself

Do remember, however, that confidence can be misplaced. In fact, over-confidence could beguile you into believing that you have a viable idea or a pleasant way of doing things when you don't. Confront your own hubris and work it out privately before it trips you up.

You work for yourself now, so you don't have to pretend about anything. In truth, you mustn't ever stray into the realms of fantasy because you would only be fooling yourself if you did.

From now on it is your job to be sensible and realistic. Do not exaggerate your potential or delude yourself that you can do all sorts of things that you cannot. Equally, do not be sheepish about your skills. You will need to get used to showing a fascinating blend of confidence and humility. It is perfectly fine to have a different external persona, but make sure that you are honest with yourself and that you know your true self.

Consider your position with extreme care and as much objectivity as you can muster.

Ask yourself:

▶ What are you good at?

▶ How much is that worth to someone else?

▶ How much will someone pay for what you have to offer?

▶ Is that enough for you to live on, or to satisfy your ambitions?

Get a piece of paper. Write down what you want to do in your business. Consider it for a while, and then decide whether anyone else would agree with you. This is the beginning of establishing whether there is indeed a market for what you do. Go for a walk. When you return, look at your piece of paper again. Is it any good? Is it nonsense? If so, write a new one. Stick it on the wall and live with it for a few days. Does it still make sense? Is it rubbish? Does everyone else claim the same thing? What's so different about the way that you would run your business?

These early enquiries are really important. They are the starting point of you being able to have a board meeting with yourself. A degree of schizophrenia here is essential. One half of your mind needs to be capable of putting forward an idea, and the other half needs to be smart enough to confirm or reject it without upsetting yourself in the process. That's no easy matter. So practise debating things on your own, weighing up the pros and cons, reaching a sensible conclusion, deciding what to do next, and remaining calm and objective throughout the whole process.

> **Remember this: Personal honesty**
>
> People do talk a lot of nonsense these days, particularly in business. Do not let this be you. Woolly thinking will give you and your business a false start, and self-deception at this stage will lead to trouble later.

# Research your market thoroughly

If you think you have an excellent idea, the first essential thing to do is to research your market thoroughly. Actually it isn't simply one thing to do – it's a lot of things. Try asking yourself these sorts of questions:

▶ What demand is there for what you provide?

▶ If you are producing a product, who wants to buy it?

▶ If you are providing a service, who needs it?

▶ Who else in the area does this already? (This could be geographical or sector-based.)

▶ Are they a success? If so, why?

▶ Are they a failure? If so, what does that tell you?

▶ What price can you put on your product or service?

▶ Does that represent a going concern or will you be hard-pushed to make a living?

▶ What outside factors are you subject to?

▶ Can you influence these factors or are you totally at their mercy?

▶ If you have no control over them, does that make the whole venture too vulnerable?

▶ If you were someone else, would you honestly embark on this venture?

▶ Why?

The questions are endless, but one of the best pieces of advice here is to be like an inquisitive child and always ask 'Why?'

three times in relation to every question. Or, if you are inclined to overstate the potential of everything because you are so enthusiastic about it, ask someone else to ask you 'Why?' in relation to all your assertions about how this venture is definitely going to be a roaring success from day one. There is absolutely nothing wrong with oodles of enthusiasm at this stage. Actually, it is an essential prerequisite if you are to be a solo success, but the business won't succeed on enthusiasm alone if it is not tempered with some good old-fashioned realism. If you are a hopeless dreamer, get the reality mongers in to check if you are heading off on a wild goose chase that could end in disaster. This will soon establish whether or not you are deluding yourself.

With the advent of seemingly endless online data sources, a huge amount can be gleaned from just sitting at your desk and letting the information pour in to your desktop. In one respect this is fine, and it is a good place to start. However, do make sure that you get out and about and talk to people. There is no substitute for talking to prospective customers, wandering about a locality, and getting a human feel for things. Strike a balance between the two.

## Work out how much money you need

This sounds obvious, but it is amazing how many people don't really cover the groundwork in this area. What is required here is not a forest of spreadsheets – just a really clear impression of how your business will work financially. Put simply, there are three types of money that you will need:

1 Investment at the start

2 Monthly cash flow

3 The profit (monthly or annual)

It is extraordinary how many businesses mess all this up. Here is the layperson's guide to the three types.

## INITIAL INVESTMENT

Let's look at the investment needed at the start.

▶ Do you need to put in any money at all at the beginning? Pause on this one for a moment. If the answer is no, then don't do it.

▶ If you do need to borrow from some other source, what demands will the lenders make on getting it back? Banks want interest. Investors want cash back. They don't lend money out of kindness. It is so easy to be seduced by the sort of macho talk that goes with establishing a business. You know the sort of stuff: 'We've got some seed corn investment from a consortium of city backers'; 'The Venture Capital guys are really interested in the idea'. This may make you feel very important, but these people want their money back, and some. And they may want to be involved in the way you run the business. Therefore, if you can do it without them, then do.

▶ If you do have to put money in yourself, when are you going to get it back? Don't delude yourself by excluding this amount from your assessment of whether the business is going to be a success.

Many self-employed people say that their business is 'successful' whilst simultaneously failing to remind themselves that 'the business' owes them thousands. This may be acceptable in the early stages, but not if there is no likelihood of you being repaid in the foreseeable future.

## MONTHLY CASH FLOW

This is the amount of income you need each month. Write down what you need. Now write down what you think you can get. Then build in time delays for late payment in the early days. This becomes your first cash-flow projection.

This projection has to be very, very realistic. You must have a reasonable level of confidence that it is achievable otherwise you will have a disaster on your hands almost immediately. You need to distinguish very carefully between income and profit. If you are ever tempted to start calling this income money 'profit', it has all gone wrong. That means it has gone wrong both on paper and in your head. To repeat, this is not profit – it is income. You can have an infinite amount of the stuff and yet still be making a whopping loss. Make sure that you make proper allowance for all the outgoings that may crop up, as well as an amount to pay yourself a salary to keep the wolf from the door.

Another massive pitfall is if you mentally earmark this money to 'mortgage' other costs. In the same way that shopaholics rationalize a purchase by saying 'I didn't spend £300 on that, so I can use it for something else', you must never double-count your money.

Calculate how much you need to make each month. Once you write it down, it is more likely to happen. (This is a general principle that works for almost everything – if you write it down it is more likely to happen.) You can have a sensible minimum and maximum, but it is better if you have just one figure. Now you have to work out where it's coming from. Write down a realistic list of the value of your income in the first three months. If this turns out to be nonsense, write a more realistic list next time. As you become better at predicting, you will naturally build in time lags to reflect slow decision making and slow payment (see Chapter 6, 'Understanding time').

### THE PROFIT (MONTHLY OR ANNUAL)
The final thing to consider is the profit margin. Ask yourself:

▶ How much is the profit?

▶ Does it vary depending on what you have sold?

▶ Does it vary by month or season?

▶ Does it fluctuate wildly?

▶ Why?

▶ What would make it more consistent?

▶ What would make it higher?

▶ What are the tolerance levels?

▶ What is the average target?

- ▶ Is that realistic?
- ▶ Is it good enough for you?

You need to keep a regular and close eye on this. You also need to have decided whether you need the profit margin monthly, annually or over any other time period.

- ▶ If you need the profit margin monthly, does this mean that your business plan does not include an amount for your own salary?
- ▶ If so, is that wise or realistic?
- ▶ If you can take the profit annually, how are you keeping tabs on the surplus that is (hopefully) building up?
- ▶ Can you equate it back to the running monthly amount?

Be aware that if you manage to convince yourself that you can wait quite a long time to realize a certain margin (a year or more), then you may well have a vulnerable business on your hands. Successful businesses make a good margin with almost everything they do, effectively from day one. Consider this carefully. There is no point in driving yourself into the ground all year only to make a few per cent, unless you are extremely happy with the figure that it generates.

The overall rule is to keep all this incredibly simple. The moment you overcomplicate the finances you will lose the plot and probably start talking nonsense about the business which, as we are beginning to realize, is one of the worst enemies of anyone working on their own. For another perspective on this whole area, have a look at one of my other books, *Start*, which includes a one-page business plan.

**Try it now: How much money?**

When looking at your start-up costs, don't take the view that you'll see how it goes. Work out what you need and make sure you can afford it. It's no good running out of money before you reap the benefit.

# Write a simple, realistic plan

Quite a few diligent sole traders write endless business plans before they start, and there is nothing fundamentally wrong with that. However, a lot of them get so involved in the spreadsheets and the financial projections that they lose sight of the basics. The best business plans can often be written on the back of an envelope, usually in your local café or bar. Try this simple process:

► Write J F M A M J J A S O N D along the top of the page to represent the 12 months of the year.

► Now cross out at least one or two of them because you will be taking some holiday, and in the first year the whole thing will probably grind to a halt when you are not around.

► Now write a figure under each month to determine your income.

► Put the likely costs under each.

► Subtract one from the other and see what you have left.

► If you want to be particularly cautious, try crossing out the first three months' income because businesses always take longer to get off the ground than you think.

► Come back to your plan and ask yourself again: 'Is this realistic?'

This exercise will tell you something more fundamental than a meeting with the bank or your accountant. It will be a big surprise if you are happy with it first time. In truth, if you are, you should be a little suspicious. Live with it for a while. Try again. Make refinements (not on a spreadsheet, just in pen on another envelope). The great joy with this is that, by keeping it simple, you are now able to explain your business plan to anyone who will listen – and that includes you. Consequently, you are less likely to drift away from your main purpose as the months and years pass by. In some business circles, they call this 'focus'. You should call it 'knowing what I am doing'.

A simple plan

| J | F | M | A | M | J | J | A | S | O | N | D |
|---|---|---|---|---|---|---|---|---|---|---|---|

X Launch date

X Hols                           X Hols

| | Income | 4 | 4 | 4 | 4 | 0 | 4 | 4 | 4 | 0 |
|---|---|---|---|---|---|---|---|---|---|---|
| | Costs | 2 | 2 | 2 | 2 | 2 | 2 | 2 | 2 | 2 |
| | Profit | 2 | 2 | 2 | 2 | -2 | 2 | 2 | 2 | -2 |

First year profit: 10

Pessimistic profit assuming no income in first 3 months: 4

Now, assuming that you have concluded that you do indeed have a going concern, there are some things that you will need to get under way.

**Try it now:** A simple plan

Write down on one sheet what you want to earn, how many sales at what price will be needed to achieve it, deduct all costs, and see if the plan works. Don't paralyse your launch by constantly reworking the figures.

# Invest in a distinctive identity

You need to look good. Your company, shop or service needs a memorable name, a good logo, high-quality headed paper, good quality signage, and business cards that invoke a reaction. The name may well be your own if you are known in your field. If not, choose something distinctive. Avoid bland sets of initials that no one can remember (such as BLTWP), or hugely cumbersome stacks of names like Jones, Duncan, Taylor, Hatstand European Consolidated & Partners. They are not memorable and they imply a lack of clarity on your part.

Every detail counts. Don't skimp on quality of paper or thickness of business cards. Thin business cards are as weak as a limp handshake. Don't have them printed at a booth in a railway station! Check the spelling and punctuation really carefully on everything you produce. These days, the world appears to be one large typographical error. Don't be part of it.

What many business people don't seem to realize is that, if there are mistakes in the way that you market your own business, many potential customers will conclude that they should not bother to do business with you. They will automatically assume that what you offer will be as shoddy as your marketing materials, and, of course, they may be right. This is not an image you want to convey.

When you are describing your business, don't tell people that you haven't really made your mind up about what you want to do, or that you are 'just giving it a go to see what happens'.

If you are indecisive about your own concern, you may well unwittingly give the impression that you will be indecisive or unreliable when dealing with your customers. And why would anyone want to do business with someone who has already said that they might not be around for very long? Customers are much more likely to be loyal to businesses that are reliable and consistent in their own right.

## Get connected

Computers are an essential element of almost every business. They are not there to ruin your life, but to make it easier. If the nature of your business is particularly artistic, or if you simply don't like computers, then you may find the whole area quite daunting. But it is essential that you get your act together at the outset otherwise you will have real problems later.

You will certainly need a computer that is dedicated solely to your business. If you mix it with your social stuff then something will go pop very quickly. I have heard of people's kids erasing business databases inadvertently. You may well want a hand-held personal organizer to complement your mobile phone, or a combined device. Approach this cautiously though. If you are receiving messages throughout the evening and cannot resist looking at them, then your relationship with your partner will suffer horribly. For a full appraisal of these dangers and how to cope with them, read another of my books, *Tick Achieve*.

You really only need 'enough' technology to be efficient and professional. Carry the personal organizer at all times during the working day so that you can give instant responses about your availability. Don't say: 'I'll get back to you.' Tell them immediately when you can meet or complete some work, and agree it on the spot. This is an essential self-employed version of the 'Think Do' management principle in which you must do something the moment you think of it. The last thing you need when you run your own business is a list of people to get back to. Do it now. It saves doing everything twice, and it makes you seem really on the ball.

Put all your information on your personal organizer and computer, and back them up regularly on disk to avoid calamity (put these back-up reminders in your diary now). Think carefully about what you want your computer to do for your business, and choose your system accordingly.

▶ What information might you want to retrieve at some point in the future?

▶ What might your customers want to know?

▶ What might you want to know?

▶ What about your accountant or the dreaded tax inspector?

▶ What is the best way of cataloguing your records?

▶ What is the simplest way of doing all this?

Do not design your system around what the technology can do. Instead, decide what you want, and design something around those needs. Some careful thought at this stage could save you hours of heartache in the future.

## Appoint a good accountant

There are whole books on this one subject, but let's stick to the basics. You really do need to know how to arrange all your financial affairs from the beginning. You won't want to discover at the end of the year that you have been recording information in the wrong way and that you now have to reorganize everything. Decide what you need, and organize all your money matters in the easiest possible way. Meeting your accountant once a year should be sufficient, with a few telephone calls every now and then to clarify any details. Keep it simple and think ahead. If you have money problems looming, address them early. Never succumb to the terrible practice of shoving bills in a problem drawer and ignoring them for months – you will create mounting debt and establish a reputation for not paying your suppliers. This is the slippery slope to bankruptcy.

Depending on the nature of your business, here are some of the gritty financial issues that must be addressed right at the beginning.

▶ Will you be a sole trader or will you register as a company at Companies House?

▶ Do you need separate bank accounts?

▶ If so, how many?

▶ How will your tax affairs be arranged?

▶ What type of National Insurance will you have to pay?

▶ Which elements of the business need to be kept financially separate?

▶ Do you need to rearrange parts of your current personal money habits to adjust to the new set-up?

▶ Do you need to register for VAT (value added tax)?

▶ What is the optimum system for paying the lowest amount of tax?

These fundamental questions need to be answered straightaway. Lots of people who work for themselves have started their first year without paying enough attention to these financial basics. At the end of their first trading year, they are then confronted by a nightmare of interrelated money matters that either cannot be undone, or cost a lot to disentangle. It is worth putting the work in now to avoid disappointment and unnecessary work in a year's time. There are many books on how to approach the technical detail, but the best thing to do is to have a frank meeting with the people who know about these things and then do exactly what they recommend before you start to generate any income.

# Work out the materials you need

You need to work out precisely what materials you need to run
your business. This sounds rather basic but you would be surprised
by the number of people who drift into their new solo life without
really knuckling down to resolve such basic questions as:

▶ If you are running a retail outlet, what stock do you need?

▶ How much investment does that involve?

▶ How quickly can you re-order?

▶ Do you know where from?

▶ Do you have the contacts?

▶ Where will stock be stored?

▶ Is it safe and secure?

▶ Is it insured?

▶ What system will you have for knowing when you are
running out of stock?

▶ Are there legal requirements that you need to take into account?

If you are selling a service, at a minimum you will need a clear
description of what you are offering cogently written down.
This might be a brochure, your CV, a client list, some examples
of your skills, and a list of things that could be of interest to a
potential customer. You will certainly need terms of business.
Most businesses start without these, and only draw some up after
their first debt. The smart person has them from the beginning to
set a precedent and to head off financial problems from the off.

We will look at some of the most important general business
tools in Chapter 3 ('Getting the money right'), but there may
be some specific to your line of work that you can work out for
yourself. Here is a basic checklist:

▶ Description of your business

▶ Your CV

▶ Your clients

► Examples of what you offer

► Examples of what you have done for others

► Prices

► Terms of business.

Whatever they are, get them organized now.

# Network constantly without being irritating

What's the difference between networking and marketing? Not that much. As a start-up business, you are unlikely to have the funds to pay for an advertising campaign or other publicity. The main burden of letting people know that you are open for business falls on you. Thus, you need to overcome any shyness or reservations you may have about marketing your business.

Have business cards on you all the time, including during social time. This is where you will pick up lots of your work. Once you start chatting, most people are interested in what you do. Without forcing your product or service on them, you can always seem professional by letting them know what you offer and having your contact details to hand. There is a huge difference between basic marketing and being irritating. Calm, professional marketers state what they do in a clear, charming way. If the reaction of the other person is reasonably positive, they might hand over a card. It's amazing how, months later, the phone can ring and a potential new customer says 'I met you once and now I have a need for what you do ...'

This is a vital hurdle to overcome, particularly if you have a shy or reticent nature. Who do you think will be the better client? The one you cold-called and had a rather earnest meeting with? Or the one you met socially who decides to give you business in their own time? Speculative business meetings are no more scientific than interviews. They are based mainly on intuition. Yet if you already know you can get on with someone socially, or that they have a little insight into your private life, the chemistry part of the equation is already in place.

A final word on social media and social networking. There are businesses where this can be very appropriate, and used as an excellent tool to promote contact, discussion and possibly business. However, it is easy to fall into the trap of twittering on your computer all day and strangely discovering that you haven't got anything done, met anybody in person, or done any business. Try to keep this in perspective. Whilst everybody else is pursuing the latest fad, make sure that you are still talking to people, having meetings, and interacting with the real, rather than just the virtual, world.

**Remember this:** Network constantly

Without being a pain, get yourself out and about. Meet socially and in a business context. Let people know what you do and that you are available for work. People can't use you if they don't know you are there.

## Now make it happen

You are now as ready as you will ever be to start your new working life. Take a little pause and reflect on all the elements you have organized:

▶ Have you thought of everything?

▶ Have you been rigorous with the issues?

▶ Have you been completely honest with yourself? (If the answer is no, you need to have a serious word with yourself because you cannot run your own business if you delude yourself.)

Do you have the energy and determination to see this thing through? (Bear in mind that you may need more resourcefulness than you think because there will always be something that you haven't thought of to trip you up.)

It is also very important to remember that, if you don't do it, it won't get done. Sitting around doing endless Venn diagrams and spreadsheets won't pay the bills. Ideas that work in theory but not in practice are not worth pursuing when you work on your own.

As the old academic joke goes:

> 'Yes, I know it works in practice, but does it work in theory?'

Time is money. It's down to you and you alone. Scary? Certainly. Exciting? Absolutely.

So if you really want an answer to the question 'Where do I start?' the answer is: 'Right here, right now'.

## Try it now: Make it happen

The world is full of moaners who think things happen to them. Sole traders cannot think like that. The good ones make things happen. Inertia ruins many a business. Now get on with it.

## Focus points

* Assume that you have something to offer.
* Be honest with yourself.
* Research your market thoroughly.
* Work out how much money you need.
* Write a simple, realistic plan.
* Invest in a distinctive identity.
* Get connected.
* Appoint a good accountant.
* Work out the materials you need.
* Network constantly without being irritating.

# 2

# The right tools for the job

In this chapter you will learn:

- ▶ *How to design your contact list*
- ▶ *How to design your new business hit list*
- ▶ *About keeping the numbers manageable*
- ▶ *How to work out what ratio of meetings generates how much work*
- ▶ *The importance of doing things when you think of them*

It would be impossible for one book to cover everything that every business needs to get launched. However, we can certainly put some essentials in place. At base level, it will be you who instinctively knows what you need in order to start your business, that is to say the tangible items such as systems, stock, premises, materials, and so on. With a little thought you can work out your computer software needs, how often you review the essentials, when to have meetings with your suppliers and business associates, and so forth. What you may not have considered in such detail are the less tangible items – the approaches and disciplines that you need to motivate yourself to get things done.

It is very much a theme of this book that the simpler things are the better they work. So in defining the right tools for the job, no attempt is made to persuade you to embark on any complicated systems or processes. In fact, the more complicated a system is, the less likely you are to get the job done. Here are the three sure-fire elements you need in order to generate a pipeline of initial business that will get you successfully launched, and enable you to keep business coming in when you have so much else to do all day.

These three really important tools will make your business a success:

**Unlock the facts: Your most important tools**

1  The contact list.
2  The new business hit list.
3  The telephone.

That's it. This is deliberately minimalist so there is no chance of you being distracted by massive spreadsheets with endless data on them. You don't want anything in the mix that wastes your time. There are many business people, and indeed consultants, who will try to convince you that you need various complicated systems to fuel your business plan. Experience suggests otherwise. The more paperwork and databases you have, the more confusion you have in the way of getting the job done. Some people love to hide behind this sort of stuff, but it doesn't work. The size of your database doesn't matter. The number of hot leads does. Piles of printouts don't matter. Two or three well-executed phone calls do. Consequently, we are going to look at these three elements and have a go at getting them under way.

# Write out your contact list and new business hit list

### THE CONTACT LIST

▶ The contact list is your lifeblood, and should be examined almost every working day.

▶ Start the first draft of the list by writing down everyone you know with whom you could possibly do business, and with whom you could get in touch.

▶ Ideally, it should only have the name of the person, the company and the date you last made contact with them on it.

▶ Don't be tempted to add other information. It will only distract you from the simple matter of picking up the telephone.

▶ If you really do feel that you need more information, write it somewhere else. Do not be tempted to enhance the list with extraneous detail – it has no bearing on the likelihood of you making the call, organizing a meeting, or achieving the thing that needs to be done, it only blurs your ability to get on with the task in hand.

▶ Every time you speak to someone or meet up with them, write the date down and move their details to the top of the list.

▶ This becomes your ready-made recall system. When you do not have anything to do, look at the very bottom of the list to see who you haven't been in touch with for some time (see Chapter 7, 'Have reserve plans for every day').

▶ Having this list basically means that you can never legitimately claim that you have nothing to do. If you ever actually find yourself believing that this is the case (very unlikely when you work on your own, but let's just suspend disbelief for the moment), then you simply go to the bottom of your contact list and call that person for a catch-up.

- If you fix a meeting or do get work as a result of that call, you might give yourself the afternoon off. That's down to you, because only you know whether you deserve it.

Example contact list

| 1 July | | |
| --- | --- | --- |
| **MEETINGS** | | |
| Roger Hughes | Hughes & Taylor | Meet 9 Jul |
| Matt Nicholls | Kaleidoscope | Meet 10 Jul |
| Sarah Taylor | Cool Corporation | Meet 15 Jul |
| **DONE** | | |
| Julie Manders | BFJW | Met 30 Jun |
| Andy Vines | Z Consortium | Spoke 28 Jun |
| Dave Jones | Zing Agency | Met 22 Jun |
| **PESTER LINE** | | |
| Rachel Davis | Mayor Management | Spoke 23 May |
| Dave Bryanston | Ball & Associates | Met 6 May |

After some months have elapsed, draw a Pester Line at a certain date when you believe it is appropriate to call the client again. If you call more than once a month, you are probably pestering, but the appropriate frequency will depend on the nature of your business. Every six months is likely to be ideal in a service business where you are involved in one or two projects a year. But if you leave it a year, many of them will have left the company or changed their job description. Work out a frequency of contact that suits the nature of your business, and adjust it if it doesn't seem to be working.

When you call a client, always say when you last spoke or met. They will be impressed by your efficiency. If you have judged the frequency right, the most likely reaction will be 'Wow, was it that long ago?' This proves that your call is timely, that it is not pestering, and that it represents an appropriate 'keep in touch' exercise.

If the client says call back on a certain date, then write the date in your personal organizer immediately, and then do it exactly when you said you would. This level of efficiency confirms that, if you do end up working for them, you will definitely deliver what you say.

The number of people on your contact list needs constant scrutiny. If there are more than 500 on the list at the outset, you are either fooling yourself or spreading yourself too thinly. It is much better to have a smaller number of viable, genuine prospects than a huge list full of people you don't really know.

Keep a constant eye on your frequency of contact. If you overdo it, after a period of receiving your (perhaps unwanted) solicitations, you will begin to tarnish your reputation (in other words, you will have overstepped the Pester Line). Or you will simply dissipate too much of your time on people who aren't interested in what you have to offer.

On the other hand, if there are fewer than 100 contacts on the list at the outset, your business may not be viable. If you were honest with yourself in Chapter 1, then you should have judged this correctly. You need a decent universe against which to apply the normal laws of probability. If you are utterly charmed, it is possible that you could sustain a living on five customers who give you precisely the amount of work that you want exactly when you need it. That's very unlikely, although it might just be feasible in a service industry where you have an established reputation that provides a ready-made flow of work.

Much more likely is a selection of potential clients who don't actually give you work despite regular promises; work which does eventually arrive but much later than you expected; projects which turn out to be much smaller than anticipated when they do eventually arrive; and so on. If you sell a product, you may to a certain degree be at the whim of various market forces, a series of random factors, and the possible effectiveness of whatever offers and promotions you decide to run. Therefore, it is better if you can generate your own pipeline to even out all these variations.

In the start-up phase of a service business, you are allowed to have only 50 contacts, but you will definitely need 100 within three months (see Chapter 6, 'Understanding time'). It is also worth considering whether your founder customers will continue to be long-standing customers and, if so, for how long. You will soon conclude that some will fall away, leaving the onus on you to develop fresh contacts. Be careful to consider this issue early, otherwise by the time you spot it in the normal run of things, you will already need the new work, and you will be dismayed by the time lag until new work materializes.

One of the most common laments of people working on their own is 'I'm too busy servicing existing customers to find new ones.' What feels like only moments later, the existing customers have moved on, and that person may well be out of business. Under no circumstances let this happen to you. It is your responsibility to become adept at running existing relationships whilst simultaneously engineering new ones. You are a plate spinner, a dextrous juggler, and a one-man band all rolled into one.

Scary but true: if you cannot generate 50 genuine contacts in the start-up phase of a service business, you should not be working on your own.

### THE NEW BUSINESS HIT LIST

Your second essential tool is the new business hit list. This is the list that you generate once your contact list has taken shape. You need to think carefully and very broadly about anyone who could have a bearing on the success of your business. This is not a cynical exercise in exploitation. It is merely casting the net as wide as possible to make the most of the potential contacts that you have.

## Unlock the facts: The value of lists

Your contact list immediately tells you whether you know enough people to make your business a success. Your new business hit list lets you know whether you have a sufficient pipeline to ensure future sales. If you don't know *who* you know, or who you *want* to know, then you can't get going.

# Write down everyone you want to get in touch with

Take your time. This list will not appear as if by magic. You need to rack your brains a bit.

▶ Don't think only of the one person you know at a company

▶ What about colleagues, bosses and assistants?

- ► Would approaching several be more advantageous than only one?

- ► Have you considered friends with interesting jobs?

- ► Have you reviewed categories where you have related experience?

- ► Have you scoured the trade press?

- ► Have you remembered all your past colleagues who have moved on to other things?

- ► Think a long way back (you may surprise yourself).

- ► Have you included those who are still at your former places of work?

- ► As a rule of thumb, the majority of people on this list should be people that you do not know, whereas by definition those on the contact list will be known to you, if only initially via a phone conversation.

**Remember this:** Get in touch

Work out your ideal customer base. Your first customers will come from this list. Don't be shy. Tell them the nature of your business and what you can do for them. If you don't tell them, they'll never know.

## Put the phone number by every one of your contacts

This may sound pedantic but human nature will dictate that if the phone number isn't by the name, it simply gives you another excuse not to make the call. You will soon realize that, when you work for yourself, making excuses is the highest form of personal insult. You are basically saying that you are happy to let yourself get away with it. Well don't! If the number is by the name, you have no excuse. Now make the calls (see Chapter 5, 'Taming the telephone').

## Do everything when you think of it, otherwise nothing will happen

This is another fantastic truism, but it really does work. Think about it. Things either are or they aren't. Have you made the call or not? When you think of something, then do it immediately. 'Think Do' is one of the most fundamental principles of the successful businessperson. Of course, you cannot do literally everything at once, but what you can do is write down everything that needs to be done in a sensible order and work your way through it.

Writing something down is in itself a doing action that helps to get things done. (For more on this, look at another of my books, *Tick Achieve*.) The great advantage that you have here is that in an office other members of staff keep interrupting you. If you are on your own, these interruptions are far less frequent so you can get a great deal more done. Ten phone calls in less than an hour? No problem.

Example new business hit list

| NAME | COMPANY | LAST SPOKE | NUMBER |
|------|---------|-----------|--------|
| **PRIORITY** | | | |
| Dave Jenks | Zebra | 11 Oct | 7234 0001 |
| Sarah Bowen | HHZ | 24 Oct | 7654 9870 |
| Richard Stokes | Fruit! | 31 Oct | 7222 0987 |
| **NEXT UP** | | | |
| Roger Batty | RB Cleaners | 10 Aug | 8675 4321 |
| Bob Hatton | Standard | 8 July | 8970 5647 |
| Mary Brooks | Dragon Design | 1 June | 7664 7865 |

## Constantly review the new business hit list to see if you are being realistic

There is no merit in generating a vast list of prospects to call only to make yourself feel good when, in truth, you are unlikely to get round to calling them all, or might not get through to many of them, let alone get work as a result. Refine your thinking regularly by asking direct questions:

- Where are you likely to have most success?
- Why is a certain approach not working?
- What new approach might work?
- How can you apply one set of skills to another market?
- Have you overlooked an obvious source of business?
- What type of work do you enjoy most?
- Where do you make the best margin?
- Which examples of previous work are most impressive?

Now start getting the list into some sort of priority order. Put the hottest prospects at the top and revise the order when things change.

## Keep the numbers manageable

Any fewer than ten numbers on your hit list and you are being lazy. How long does it take to make ten phone calls? Less than an hour, which of course means that you cannot claim that you don't have the time. Any more than 50 and you will faze yourself and do nothing, rather like facing a plate with too much food on it. If you have trouble tackling a list of this size, break it down into manageable chunks that suit you. Groups of six or ten perhaps. Try colour-coding them so that you can distinguish one set from the other.

And if your first system doesn't work, simply admit it and invent a new one. Remember, any system is entirely for your own convenience and you don't have to discuss it with anyone else. Just make it work for you.

## Keep inventing new ideas for contacting someone

You need to be vigilant about issues and trends. Pick up on articles in the trade press. Track movements of people and ideas. It works well when you ring up and say that you have noticed something relevant to them and have a suggestion. It shows that you are on the ball, and makes it easier to get work.

If you are selling products, keep re-analysing their appeal to your customer base.

▶ What is 'in' at the moment?

▶ Do your products fit that mood?

▶ Can you extend your range?

▶ What if you run a promotion?

▶ What if you alter your pricing?

▶ How about some local marketing?

▶ Are your marketing materials out of date or looking a little tired?

▶ Are there any seasonal events that you should be capitalizing on?

### Try it now: New contact ideas

Just because someone didn't buy your first suggestion doesn't mean they won't buy your second. Things change all the time. Bright ideas appropriately suggested are always interesting to people. Keep coming up with new ones.

## Every time you get through to someone, move them to your contact list

The definition of a contact is a meeting or a proper phone conversation. At bare minimum you will have explained who you are, provided your details and discussed the possibility of work at some point in the future. Never have someone on your contact list who should be on your new business hit list. This would be deluding yourself. They are not a genuine contact until you have spoken to them properly or met them and discussed at least the vague possibility of working together at some point in the future.

# Try to have 20–30 meetings fixed for the next 4–6 weeks

In the early days, you need to pull out all the stops to generate some critical mass. That means a lot of meetings and probably a lot of coffee. Keep the meetings short and get to the point. You are a busy person and so are they. Never book more than four half-hour meetings in a day. You will lose energy and become bored of describing what you do.

Two a day is ideal. Later on, when you have some paying customers, you can reduce this number and be more choosy. But to start with, there is no substitute for putting in the hard work.

The mathematics of this is discussed in more detail in Chapter 5, 'Taming the telephone', but the basics are as follows:

▶ The amount of business you think you currently have probably won't be enough.

▶ Something unexpected will happen, so you need contingency income.

▶ The law of averages will ensure that you will only get a percentage of the business you are aiming for.

▶ So you need to work out your strike rate.

▶ The number of contacts you need in order to fuel your business will be significantly greater than the number of customers or projects that you actually need to run a viable business.

▶ You have to overcompensate, particularly in the start-up phase.

**Try it now:** Fix those meetings

It's no use waiting for the mountain to come to Mohammed. There is no substitute for meeting, talking and suggesting ideas. That's how you'll get your customers.

# Never cancel a new business meeting because you are 'too busy'

'I'm sorry, I can't make it because I have too much on.'

This is a classic mistake that many people make. If you think about it carefully, you will realize that the person you are talking to could make a number of assumptions. If you are incredibly lucky, they will be impressed that you are so much in demand. But the more likely reaction is that you are a one-man band who is unable to cope. Which means that you certainly won't be able to handle whatever they might have in mind. Goodbye project! You may never get the meeting again, so you should say yes, and work harder for a brief period.

## THE TELEPHONE

The telephone is the third essential string to your bow, and we are going to get to grips with it in Chapter 5 ('Taming the telephone'). If you have a particular issue with 'cold calling' or any other aspect of phoning people, you might want to read that chapter now. If not, don't worry for the moment. It's not nearly as daunting as you may think. Meanwhile, assuming that you have successfully established your two lists, you have the right tools for the job and you are ready to do business.

**Remember this:** Never cancel

If you cancel a new business meeting – for any reason – you may never get the meeting back in the diary. Many a business has fallen by the way because they were apparently too busy with existing work to look for future customers. This is the oldest trap in the book, so don't fall into it.

### Focus points

* ✻ Write out your contact list and new business hit list.
* ✻ Write down everyone you want to get in touch with.
* ✻ Put the phone number by every one of them.
* ✻ Do everything when you think of it.
* ✻ Constantly review the list to see if you are being realistic.
* ✻ Keep the numbers manageable.
* ✻ Keep inventing new ideas for contacting someone.
* ✻ Every time you get through to someone, move them to your contact list.
* ✻ Try to have 20–30 meetings fixed for the next 4–6 weeks.
* ✻ Never cancel a new business meeting because you are 'too busy'.

# 3

# Getting the money right

In this chapter you will learn:

- ▶ *How to concentrate on the money, but not become obsessed with it*
- ▶ *How to weigh up the service v product distinction*
- ▶ *About the lucky seven money questions*
- ▶ *How to work out the price–quality equation*
- ▶ *About Everyday Flexible Pricing*

Whatever you do to make a living, and no matter how much you absolutely love it, there is no point in doing it unless you make a sensible amount of money for the effort you put in. You really owe it to yourself to get the money side of things right. So how exactly do we set about doing that?

## Concentrate on the money, but don't become obsessed with it

The dreaded money. The filthy lucre. Yes, it's true. From now on, when you discuss money, it will not be in some abstract way based on a remote budget that was agreed by someone you have never met. It will be a highly personal matter. Have you ever noticed how company people talk about budgets, allocations and fiscals? They often adopt a rather blasé manner. They even say 'ten k' instead of 10,000! Once you have earned £10,000 entirely off your own bat, it is extremely unlikely that you will ever use the letter 'k' in that way again.

From now on, every time you discuss money it will all be your personal money, so you'd better start concentrating harder. It has been said that you don't really appreciate what running your own business means until you have experienced a bad debt, so it is essential that you become comfortable talking about money straightaway. If you don't, you will probably agree to produce unspecified amounts of work over unclear time periods, and in some instances you might not get paid at all.

Alternatively, you may consistently sell products at margins so low that your business will not be viable. Although this sounds incredibly obvious, huge numbers of businesspeople pursue a large volume of sales so that they can brag about the scale of their operation. They crow about turnover, but frequently they are barely making a profit. There is no merit whatsoever in rushing around all year creating things to do when you aren't actually making money. It doesn't make any sense. Therefore, address this by keeping a very close eye on your margin, and by constantly questioning why you are doing what you are doing.

**Remember this: Don't obsess over the numbers**

If you are working properly, the numbers will take care of themselves. Work out a rough shape of what the business requires, and then get on with it. Wandering round with a spreadsheet all day won't get the business working.

# Weigh up the Service v Product distinction

It is extremely difficult to give general guidelines about how to handle money without distinguishing between service- and product-based businesses. If you produce or sell any form of product, then the basic equation of your business will be based on the cost of making or acquiring it in relation to the amount for which you sell it. That's your margin or, put another way, 'materials with mark-up'. These businesses are almost always less profitable than service businesses that can attribute an acceptable price for an idea or a thing done (unless the manufacturer of that product has such enormous economies of scale that the amount of cash coming in makes the point irrelevant).

Of course this is a sweeping generalization, but it stands to reason that it is usually easier for a potential customer to attribute a perceived value to a tangible item than it is to an intangible one. Moreover, services and ideas can often cost nothing other than your time and talent to create. Consequently, in theory the price of a service or idea is limitless, whereas that of an item probably has a limit beyond which the market is unlikely to go. Consider this principle in relation to your own business. Ask yourself:

▶ What level of mark-up will your customers accept?

▶ What can you do to make what you provide worth more?

▶ Do you have enough services on offer to increase your average margin?

▶ Is your pricing appropriate for what you provide?

# Work out how to have a near-infinite margin

If you run a service business, you should consider resisting the temptation to have offices, a partner, a secretary and any other baggage. You may be able to operate without them. Before you tear off and spend a fortune on things that you may not actually need, look at these questions.

### Unlock the facts: A near-infinite margin?

Can you offer something that relies purely on your skill or experience? If so, there could be a goldmine lurking in it. Start by thinking of the simplest thing that people might pay you for, and that requires as little investment and resources as possible.

# Consider the lucky seven money questions

**The lucky seven money questions**

1  Could you do without offices by working from home?

2  If you cannot work from home, is there an elegant alternative?

3  Could you operate without a formal business partner?

4  Could you have fewer prescribed arrangements where you can bring contacts in as and when work dictates?

5  Could you survive without delegating anything?

6  With a little ingenuity and re-engineering, could you do everything you need yourself?

7  Could you pay yourself less for a while?

If the answer is yes to all of these, you can have a near-infinite margin. Of course, there are always those who claim that the sociability and interaction provided by an office environment are essential to the way they work. Fair enough. But you can imitate the important elements of these circumstances in almost every way by having plenty of meetings, bouncing ideas off friends and having a decent social life. In fact, being self-employed should massively improve your social reliability. For once in your life, you have no silly commute and no boss forcing you to stay at the office, so you can have much more enterprising free time on your own terms. You will probably live longer and have fewer medical bills as well.

## Try to avoid the most time-consuming business issue ever: other people

Ever heard of 'high maintenance' members of staff? This is because one of the most time-consuming issues in any business is other people. No one is suggesting that you become a hermit, and perhaps your business genuinely cannot function without a workforce. However, if you are working for yourself, you do at least have the option to consider structuring a business that minimizes the effect others can have on your fortunes. You owe it to yourself to consider whether there is any possibility that you could run your business without anyone else. If there is any chance that you might, it is a strongly recommended option. Why? Because when you are on your own you:

▶ Make clearer decisions

▶ Make faster decisions

▶ Do business in your own unique style

▶ Avoid having to deal with politics

▶ Do not have to feel guilty about relationships with colleagues

▶ Can experience a truly direct link between effort and reward.

## Try to sell what you do, not materials with a mark-up

There are many other things that can make an enormous difference to your profitability. Your talents theoretically have a limitless price. That means that, within certain sensible parameters, you can charge what you want. Materials are finite and have an approximate known price, so they can usually be undercut by a competitor and thus decrease your margin. The smartest sole traders do not sell materials or any fixed price service. They sell experience and ideas. This is not a way to rip off customers – quite the opposite. The most powerful question you can ask is:

*'If I fix x, what is it worth to your business?'*

The answer to this question is quite fascinating. Some potential customers will not have the foresight to estimate (or, in their eyes, speculate wildly) what they might gain by engaging your services. In which case, they won't answer the question or will not be prepared to say that the answer might be quite a large figure. This means that they are either not a genuine potential customer or that they will be a penny-pinching bad one, which means that you should not be pursuing their business anyway.

An enlightened potential customer will rapidly be able to put a likely figure on what they stand to gain (or not lose) from your involvement, and they will be big enough to tell you the true amount. Once you get into honest conversations of this type, you can forge a direct link between your price and the customer benefit. After a number of similar conversations, you may well have enough evidence and confidence to double your prices.

### Unlock the facts: Materials with mark-up?

Material products have price points that are easier for the customer to guess accurately. They won't mind paying a certain mark-up, but there will be a limit. Services, however, can be priceless. Could you offer a premium service and have greater control over your pricing and profit?

## The price–quality equation: if you cost a lot, you must be good

What do you deduce about two products of similar type, one of which costs £2,000 and the other £200? The more expensive is probably better made and so of higher quality. It may have a cachet or brand value to which potential buyers aspire. There is nothing wrong with it being more expensive, assuming that there are people who appreciate those qualities and are prepared to pay for it. No matter how disparaging one chooses to be about products and services that are 'expensive', one is eventually forced to admit that, one way or another, there must be a market for them otherwise they would not remain in their market.

In which case, what would you deduce about two people, one of whom commands a fee of £2,000 a day, and the other £200? The more expensive is likely to be more experienced and therefore of higher quality. This is self-fulfilling, because if they are not, then in a fairly short space of time they will not generate any repeat business, and will fail as a business reasonably quickly.

It may be something of a rhetorical question, but which of these two people would you rather be? Obviously it is a hypothetical example and the gap between the two figures doesn't really matter, but the principle probably does. Far too many people who work on their own undercharge for their services, and it is often a mystery why. Nervousness certainly plays a part. Lack of confidence contributes too. And many will claim that if they put their prices up, they will either lose or fail to gain work. But if you think it through carefully, you will pretty much always look enviously upon someone who is successful in a particular field and come to the following conclusion:

*'If they cost a lot, then they must be good.'*

This is, of course, the reaction that you should aspire to invoke in your customers and competitors. Clearly there has to be an appropriate balance between price and delivery but, in the main, you should always place the maximum possible value on what you have to offer. If you are uncertain about what that value is, you need to test your pricing first. One of the lovely things about being self-employed is that you can effectively reinvent yourself and what you offer every day. If yesterday's formula didn't work, try another today. Now consider putting your prices up, and be prepared to turn work down if customers want it too cheap.

Your central maxim should be: Charge a premium price and do a great job.

## Aim for 50 per cent repeat business within three years

If this aim frightens you, there is something wrong with your ambitions. Do you expect your customers to be pleased with the work that you do? If the answer is yes, which it certainly should be, then you should expect further work in due course. If you are selling products, there is still a service element to what you do, and your objective must be to have your customers coming back. Even accounting for the random availability of projects, seasonal factors and the cyclical nature of certain markets, you should always aspire to get more business from at least half of your existing customers.

You should also track satisfied customers when they move house, move to new jobs or have a change of circumstances. Whatever has happened, they will be confronted by a whole new set of issues, many of which you may be able to address. In a service business in particular, it is important to go and have a coffee with people when they move. It is flattering for them, it gives you a flavour of their new set-up, and there is always something new to discuss.

Of course aiming for 50 per cent could be criticized as banal. Who in their right mind would aim for a percentage? It is merely a figure that will fluctuate anyway depending on the size and shape of the other elements in your business. What should make sense though are the parameters above and below which repeat purchase levels should not rise or fall. If you have 100 per cent repeat business, then the corollary is that you have no new business. This is not good. If you have no repeat business, then you would certainly be worried about the quality and value of what you produce and the long-term prospects for your business, if only judged by word of mouth recommendation and customer satisfaction. And if you had a fantastic run of new business, then you would not mind at all if your repeat percentage fell. Perhaps we should conclude that the percentage should be no lower than 30 per cent and no higher than 70 per cent in any given year.

## Don't be small-minded about money

Think big. Remember that you will probably have to type all your own invoices and do your own VAT return, so don't waste time with bits and pieces that don't get you anywhere. When quoting and invoicing, stick to units of hundreds or thousands of pounds. It is difficult to generalize here, but the basic rule is not to mess about with small fractions that do not really add to your profit, but which infuriate you when doing the books. Keep it simple and round the figures up or down (preferably up) in order to get the job done quickly and efficiently. In some instances you may lose a little on price, and in others you may gain a little, but you will save hours of fiddling about with pounds and pence or dollars and cents.

This is an extension of the 'successful people buy in bulk' principle, and applies to anyone who works on their own. Successful business people buy in bulk so that they don't have to waste time perpetually buying individual small units of a given item. This applies to pretty much everything: paper, paper clips, printer cartridges, stamps, envelopes – that rather irritating list of stuff that has to be done but doesn't really seem to have a bearing on anything. Time-wasters (who are never successful working on their own) repeat the process mindlessly again and again, usually failing to notice that the time spent on constantly doing this is detracting from their ability to do much more rewarding and profitable things. Put another way: have you heard the one about the person who never got anything done because they kept writing out lists of 'Things to do'?

Expenses are a case in point. No matter what your business, do not be petty about expenses. If at all possible, you should never charge them to the customer. If appropriate, build a suitable margin into your prices to allow for any extra services that you would normally wish to provide them. In a service business, be generous and broadminded. Buy the client lunch, and pay for your own travel. Simply get on with it in a way that befits a well-paid successful person.

Here is just one example. If you find yourself producing estimates for jobs that go into tiny detail and try to justify your every movement, you have probably either got the wrong pricing or the wrong type of customer. What a lot of people who work for themselves forget is that discussing the trivia takes as much time as talking about the important things. It therefore costs just as much money, but as a proportion of the value of the lower priced job, the time spent will probably not be viable. Therefore, be very careful not to become dragged into the mire of discussing tiny financial details whilst all the time you are missing the main point. If a customer becomes too uptight about a job and will not agree what you deem to be a fair and honest price for a job well done, walk away from the job. You are better than that.

Furthermore, don't forget that your accountant can make allowances for all sorts of things, and tidy up all the details at the end of the year. That's what you pay them for.

## Be canny about requests for free or 'win only' work

'Share in our success or failure' was one of the worst traits of the dotcom boom in the late 1990s. This is a euphemism for 'I won't pay for anything unless things have gone really well and I decide that I can afford it.' The main rule is never to give anything away for free, unless you have an overwhelming reason to do so. When people ask why you won't do speculative work, the best answer is 'Because I don't need to'. They really have no response to that.

Although there is usually no reason to give your time away for free, you do of course reserve the right to charge less or provide free work if you deem that it is appropriate.

You should try not to, but you are the best judge of any given state of affairs, and the joy of working on your own is that you do not have to discuss it with anyone else. Here are some possible reasons why you might want to provide something free or at a reduced price:

▶ Because it will lead to repeat business.

▶ Because it will lead to new business.

▶ Because it is part of a much bigger deal.

▶ Because they are a highly valued customer.

▶ Because you can.

A final thought on free work. If you have had a really good year, why not offer to work free for a charity or a worthy cause for a limited period? Your expertise may be worth significantly more than any donation you might ordinarily make, and skills are often more useful than cash. No money needs to change hands, and you can add their name to your client list and use it as part of your sales patter.

## Consider Everyday Flexible Pricing

Here's a slightly radical idea that is not for the faint-hearted: Everyday Flexible Pricing. Each day when you work on your own is effectively the beginning of a new financial year. You can state your prices any way you like, describe your background as you see fit, and accept or decline work on a whim. It really is entirely down to you. Which means you could double your prices tomorrow if you like.

This may or may not be a good idea in your market. However, you could certainly test two pricing levels side by side to see whether it has any bearing on the success of a deal. Or you could steadily increase your prices as your confidence, experience and flow of work increases. For example, if you are discussing a project that is very similar to one you have just done, increase the price by as much as you think suits, probably somewhere between 10 and 50 per cent. If the client accepts, then this becomes your new price for an exercise of that type.

Over time, this should fuel an ever-upward value equation for your business. One word of warning though: if you do try this, make absolutely sure that you know which prices you have quoted, and to whom, otherwise you may lose the plot and come across as though you are making it up as you go along. Which, of course, would be the truth.

## Try it now: Everyday Flexible Pricing

The brilliant thing about being a sole trader is that you can change your mind every day. If you achieve a certain (non-discounted) price for something today, then consider charging more for it next time. If you succeed, you might immediately improve your fortunes and set a new level of profitability for your business.

## Focus points

✳ Concentrate on the money, but do not become obsessed with it.
✳ Weigh up the Service v Product distinction.
✳ Work out how to have a near-infinite margin.
✳ Consider the lucky seven money questions.
✳ Try to avoid the most time-consuming issue ever: other people.
✳ Try to sell what you do, more so than materials with a mark-up.
✳ Examine the price–quality equation: If you cost a lot, you must be good.
✳ Do not be small-minded about money.
✳ Be canny about requests for free or 'win only' work.
✳ Consider Everyday Flexible Pricing.

# 4

# How to communicate effectively

In this chapter you will learn:

- ▶ *How to choose the right communication method*
- ▶ *To become adept at describing what you do in 30 seconds*
- ▶ *How to introduce some humanity into your CV*
- ▶ *Why it is important to meet lots of people and to stay open-minded*
- ▶ *To pay attention to customers and ask them what they want*

Communication. This must surely be one of the most complicated issues in life, let alone in a business context. Where would we be without communication? Humans cannot exist without it. Almost everything we do involves the need for it. And yet often we really aren't very good at it. So let's have a look at some of the methods at our disposal, and work out how best to use them.

## Choose the right method of communicating

Methods of communicating are constantly changing. Up until relatively recently you could only really talk to someone in person, by telephone or by writing them a letter. That was about it. You might have faxed someone or sent a courier to speed things up a little. Then came the internet and mobile telephony, and the whole scene changed. We now require a much broader set of communication skills, and we need to put much more thought into what is the appropriate method for any particular situation. We can try to put these options into some sort of hierarchy.

Here is a rank order of possible communication methods, based on (a) the likelihood of you being correctly understood and (b) probable sales success as a result:

1  Talking face to face

2  Telephone conversation

3  Letter

4  Email

5  Text message.

With regard to effectiveness, option number one must beat all the rest by a hundred to one. Consequently, if at all possible, only conduct your important business face to face. However, this is not an excuse for endorsing a 'meetings culture' in which legions of earnest businesspeople sit in meetings all day without really knowing why. Quite the opposite in fact. It is perfectly feasible to conduct meetings in a brisk, polite way that acknowledges the fact that most people are busy. Come in, get to the point, agree what is to be done, and get out. Half an hour is the ideal length for a business meeting.

Having a good telephone conversation can also be highly productive. Nevertheless, there is a huge difference between a telephone conversation with someone you have not met in person as opposed to one with someone whom you can picture. Everything is easier if you have met, so if it is important, make sure that you do indeed meet. Have a look at Chapter 5 ('Taming the telephone') for all sorts of ways to make your phone conversations more pleasant.

Letter writing is next down the list, but a very long way behind. In the direct marketing industry, the average response rate to letters is around 2 per cent. It wouldn't be much use if you only got through to two out of every 100 of your prospects, so letters have to serve a very distinct purpose. If you know that the recipient likes to have things written down, then a letter makes sense. If you have done a lot of research into the potential reader and you have a carefully argued and quite bespoke proposal, then a letter may work, particularly if it is followed by an appropriately timed phone call.

And so we come to the dreaded email. In many respects, this method has completely revolutionized our lives. Certainly, many people who work on their own could not succeed without it because of its fantastic ability to deliver things quickly and its power to enable them to stay in touch. The internet has also facilitated the transfer of much more information, and access to all sorts of data that would previously have been cumbersome and costly to obtain.

I have deliberately left off the main list social media, webinars, LinkedIn, Twitter and all the other developments that are part of online communication. The reason for this is that, although they involve communication in the broad sense, they lack the specificity of a clear business sales channel. They are more conversational than directional, and need to be regarded with caution in case you find that you have spent all day chatting when you should have been selling or doing.

As a high-quality communication method, email leaves much to be desired. Why? Because:

▶ Anything you send can be totally ignored.

▶ The presentation style is mainly in the hands of the receiver, not you.

▶ Most messages are not checked, so that any errors can make you look unprofessional or ignorant.

▶ People you don't know about are sometimes blind copied on the original for political purposes that you know nothing about.

▶ Your original message or reply is often forwarded to someone you know nothing about.

▶ Response rates for emails have plummeted to the depths of junk mail – typically 2 per cent. So if you send 100 out, you may only get two replies.

The sort of chaos that can ensue from these possibilities shouldn't really require any further elaboration. Suffice it to say that any communication method that has these pitfalls needs to be treated with extreme caution. It is perfectly fine to bat emails back and forth with a known customer who likes the method, but otherwise it is unlikely to be the method by which you grow your business. E-user beware!

 **Try it now:** The right communication method

People so often get this wrong. What is the most appropriate medium to use to speak to a customer? Face-to-face, phone, email, letter? Some careful thought will always lead to a better result. So think before you dive in.

# Become adept at describing what you do in less than 30 seconds

Lethologica is an inability to recall words. This is not something that you would ever want to suffer from. Now that you work on your own you need to improve your word power so that you are very proficient at explaining what you do. Potential customers may be interested for a maximum of one minute. This is true at an interview, a drinks party, in the pub, at the squash club – anywhere in fact. After that, they become bored. You need to get your act together and come across in a lucid, enthusiastic way.

Start by writing down what you do in no more than three sentences. Now read it out loud. Does it sound daft? If so, rewrite it. Try again. Does it sound like a cliché? Does it sound like all the other waffle you read in corporate brochures or hear from politicians on the television? If so, change it. Make it fun and engaging. Do it with some pride and a lot of energy. Excellent. Now you can use it for face-to-face conversations, telephone calls and all your written work. Also bear in mind that this should evolve constantly to keep pace with the manner in which your business develops.

**Remember this:** Describing what you do

Broadly speaking, no one cares what you do to earn a living. It's your job to express it clearly so everyone can understand and, ideally, to make it interesting and appealing. If you can't, why should anyone else bother to try to understand it?

## Be prepared to improvise on the spot

Life's a mess. Make it up as you go along! One of the joys of running your own business is that you can change the rules any time you like – several times a day if you are feeling particularly mischievous. There's nothing more boring than someone who repeats the company mantra in a soulless manner, so go with the flow a little. If you spot an opportunity, try out a sales angle. If you have a random thought, say it. If you want to discuss an idea without necessarily proposing it, then do so. It's vibrant and fun.

## Introduce some humanity into your CV

You've all seen the type of thing:

> *'Relentlessly successful, moved from A to B to C, married with two children, enjoys theatre and music.'*

That's the gist of the average CV. What can we deduce about this individual? Are they extremely reliable or just really boring? The best that we can guess is that they are a fairly steady individual. Let's compare them with the next one:

> *'Gained experience doing X, transferred skills to different industry Y, broke away and set up on own doing Z, plays in a rock band, flies birds of prey at the weekends, amateur artist and occasional cartoonist.'*

Who would you prefer to have a drink with? Who would you rather do business with?

You get the idea. If you introduce some humanity into your business life, interesting things start to happen. First, you get to know your customers so much better, not because you are asking inane questions such as 'Did you have a good weekend?', but because you really get to know what they are up to, and in most cases people do some very interesting and enterprising things that they never mention unless you ask. Second, if you work in the type of business where it is appropriate to overlap your work and social life, the whole thing becomes a pleasure instead of a chore. Third, smart customers deduce very quickly that if you are enterprising in your spare time, you probably are in your working time as well. Finally, mentioning your hobbies and outside interests can give you that extra element of pride in your achievements that is crucial to anyone who works on their own. There's nothing wrong with drawing satisfaction from your hobbies as well as your work and transferring that confidence between the two whenever you need it.

 **Try it now: Introduce some humanity into your CV**

Business CVs are dull. Many businesses are dull. Which are more interesting: your work or leisure activities? There are probably many competitors who do exactly the same as you. The difference is you. So let them know what you would be like to work with.

## Remember that people give business to those with whom they like having meetings

In Chapter 8 ('Meetings can be fun') we will discuss meetings in detail, but for the purposes of good communication you need to acknowledge what meetings are for in the first place:

► To establish a relationship

► To propose something

► To agree something.

That's about it really, and unless anything is incredibly complicated, you should be able to do what is necessary in less than an hour, and preferably less. If you are the sort of person who waffles, who has meetings without really knowing why, who doesn't prepare, and who fails to bring new ideas and proposals with them, you will be quite tedious to have meetings with. This is not a favourable impression to create. You need to be really on the ball. Don't set up meetings for the sake of it. Always ask yourself: 'What's the point?' Be sharp and lively, and establish a reputation as a person with whom a meeting is always a pleasure. You want your customers to be saying: 'Whenever I have a meeting with you I get something out of it.'

## Meet lots of people and stay open-minded

Let's spend a moment or two discussing the difference between networking and meeting lots of people. Over time you can become quite good at working out the difference between the two. When you start out, you do actually need to meet quite a lot of people. This is because the law of averages proves that you need a reasonable critical mass of contacts to make any business work. In the early days, the shape of your business will not be sharply defined (no matter how rigorous you were in the planning stages), so you need to stay open-minded.

Moreover, bear in mind that every meeting you have involves a judgement of character as well as an assessment of someone's technical skills. The more people you communicate with, the more experience you will have of working out whether you will get on well with them, and whether they will be relevant to your aspirations for your business. Once you have met, you need to keep a close eye on what happens next. Try asking yourself these types of questions:

▶ Did they send through the thing that they said they would in the meeting?

▶ Did they call in two weeks' time as they promised?

▶ Did they give my details to their colleague as we agreed?

▶ Did they consider my proposal and give me a response?

If the answer to any of these is yes, you may be on to a decent working relationship. If the answer is mainly no, you need to consider carefully whether the person is a time-waster or someone who usually fails to do what they say they will. If this proves to be the case, they will not be fulfilling to do business with and, if they are an associate of any kind, be aware that their poor approach will reflect badly on you.

Once you have met a number of people, you can refine your approach into some proper networking. This is not a cynical process whereby you extract all the benefits from people and give them nothing back. In some quarters, the very word 'networking' has as bad a reputation as 'sales'. Properly executed networking should benefit everyone. Let's define the difference between meeting many people and networking. In the early days, you need to meet lots of people and stay open-minded. When you have built up some experience of their capabilities and your aspirations, you can network. This will involve keeping in contact with those who could benefit from your skills and vice versa, at a frequency that is appropriate to your line of work and how busy they are. You keep in touch, help them out, suggest things and, ideally, do business together. Everyone wins.

# Take your customers to lunch and insist on paying

It could be lunch. It could be breakfast, dinner, the races or even just a drink. The details don't matter. The thing is that social surroundings promote a totally different mood than those of a meeting room, many of which appear to be designed precisely to reduce the chances of meetings being enjoyable. Suggesting a social get-together is a constructive, magnanimous thing to do. What does it say about you? It says that:

▶ You are broad-minded.

▶ You are interested in other aspects of your customers than their money.

▶ You can afford it.

Therefore, you will be engineering a situation in which you can show your generosity, your interest in the client, and quite possibly the degree to which you are on the ball with your suggestions of places to go and things to do.

What do you talk about when you meet up? A bit of business, certainly. But mainly simply ask short, open-ended questions and then shut up. You'll be amazed what comes up. People will talk when they are put at ease. They will talk about their families and relationships, their concerns, their feelings about their job, sport, hobbies, current affairs – pretty much anything. Of course there are some bores in the world, but in the main there are interesting things to learn and discuss. The more ideas you have, the smarter you will appear, not because you are faking it but because it will be true. It's all part of honing good communication skills.

# Rewrite all your marketing materials

Assuming that you do succeed in creating a dynamic environment for your business, things will probably change quite rapidly and so should the manner in which you describe what you do. The chances are that your marketing materials will become obsolete pretty quickly. So update them. It doesn't have to be an expensive exercise if you stick to the basics and concentrate on the elements that work well in your market.

Get out all the stuff that you have had done and spread it out on a large table. Ask yourself some questions:

▶ What do you think of the materials?

▶ Do they accurately represent what you do these days?

▶ Which bits worked and which didn't?

▶ What can you learn from that?

▶ Do you use some elements more than others?

▶ Has the emphasis of your business changed?

▶ Is there any point in producing something new?

 **Try it now:** Rewrite your marketing materials

What you said about your business two months ago might not be how you would phrase it now. Just because a marketing initiative didn't work before doesn't mean it won't work now. If your business develops fast, your existing material is probably out of date, so re-examine it.

# Design a clever mailing to send to your customers

It's amazing the number of businesses that send out one launch mailing and then sit back thinking that they have 'done marketing'. Oh dear. The market is changing all the time. People come and go. Products and tastes change. You can never conclusively prove that something that didn't work before won't work now.

Consider the merits of sending out a new mailing to your customers:

▶ What would you say?

▶ Have you ever done it before?

▶ Did you learn anything?

▶ Who would you send it to?

▶ Existing customers for repeat purchase?

▶ Or new potential customers? If so, where will you get their details?

I use the word 'mailing' in its broadest context. Choose your medium carefully. You may choose to use different media for different messages. Whatever you do, don't just fire off an email to all your contacts and assume that the business will roll in.

## Ask your customers what else you could do for them

How many businesses plough on churning out the same old stuff, assuming that what they provide is what their customers want? Most people don't like change unless someone else does all the work and makes it a pleasure. Then they can opt in or out on their own whim and in their own time. Unfortunately, when you work on your own, that someone is you. It is your job to stay very close to your customers and the markets in which you operate.

When you have some new ideas that you want to test, or even if you have none at all (hopefully not, otherwise you may be lacking the entrepreneurial spirit shown by most people who work on their own), talk to your customers. Ask them:

▶ What else could I do for you?

▶ Did you realize that what I do for you is only a fraction of what I do for some of my other customers?

▶ How much does what I do make a difference to your business?

▶ What are the main things preoccupying you at the moment?

- Would you like me to investigate something new for you?

- Are you dissatisfied with any suppliers who provide similar services to me?

- Do you know any other potential customers who might want to use my services?

- What could I do better?

By now you will know that when you ask such open-ended questions, it is your job to shut up and pay attention. The new selling opportunities are always lurking in the answers given. Let the clients talk. In many instances, your customers will invent new work for you on the spot. Occasionally drop in new ideas. Offer to develop a thought into a proposal. Suggest that you do a little development work on a subject and call them next week to see if it is worth proceeding. In the modern business world they call this being proactive. In truth it is simply having ideas and getting things done.

## Focus points

✻ Choose the right method of communicating.
✻ Become adept at describing what you do in less than 30 seconds.
✻ Be prepared to improvise on the spot.
✻ Introduce some humanity into your CV.
✻ People give business to those with whom they like having meetings.
✻ Meet lots of people and stay open-minded.
✻ Take your customers to lunch and insisted on paying.
✻ Rewrite all your marketing materials.
✻ Design a clever mailing to send to your customers.
✻ Ask your customers what else you could do for them.

# 5

# Taming the telephone

In this chapter you will learn:

- ▶ *To overcome fears and prejudices about cold calling*
- ▶ *How to understand the relationship between the number of calls and the eventual amount of work*
- ▶ *How to prepare your selling angles*
- ▶ *A system for noting your calls*
- ▶ *The ten golden rules of unsolicited calling*

The phone is a two-way machine that can be a great asset or an object that invokes considerable fear. Many people hate what they describe as 'cold calling'. If you are one of them, and particularly if you are in a service business, you need to address this issue urgently and befriend your phone. Once you get the hang of it, it's really not as bad as you think.

With regard to the telephone, there are certain matters that anyone who runs their own business needs to confront. Start by reading this chapter and try to apply some of the suggestions. Whatever you do, don't reject the idea before you have a go – it is not nearly as onerous as many would have you believe.

# Don't call it 'cold calling'

Who said cold calling was cold? Rarely has an activity been so badly titled. Calling someone on the phone is usually a very pleasant thing to do. Even in business. In reality, those who view it as cold calling are probably cold themselves, and are not that keen on other people anyway. It is far better to view the whole process as just calling someone for a chat. The fact that you have never met that person has nothing to do with it. If you are charming and have something interesting to say, it will be a pleasure for both sides. You wouldn't hesitate to call a friend, and sometimes you might even call them without a reason. In business, there is always a reason, so all you have to do is state clearly what the reason is and get to the point.

There are many ideas here about how to get the conversation started and overcome the initial hurdles. However, they will work to a lesser degree until you get to grips with the emotional barriers and convince yourself that it really isn't such a big deal to pick up the phone, and that great things can happen once you take the plunge. One way to do this is to consider all the worst things that could possibly happen if things don't go as well as you hoped. Here are some examples:

## ▶ They say they are not interested in what you do

So what? This is very valuable information. Lots of people spend weeks, months, years even, pursuing someone who simply isn't interested in what they have to offer, and never will be. This could be an individual or a company whose culture doesn't suit yours and vice versa. Take it on the chin and move on.

### ▶ They refuse to take your call

This is most interesting. If someone spends the bulk of their time hiding behind a barrage of secretaries and assistants, there are two things you can deduce about them. Either they may be genuinely busy, or they enjoy creating the impression that they are busy. If it is the former, then it doesn't mean that they are not interested in what you do. Either keep trying or use a different method of getting in touch that suits their style better. If it is the latter, think carefully about whether you would really like to do business with them. Will they be a badly behaved customer? Will they respond to your calls if you do end up working together? Will they pay you on time? And there are a host of other issues that could make your life a misery. 'Only do business with people you like' is a maxim that will serve you well.

### ▶ They are rude or dismissive

This is a bit unpleasant but no less helpful than either of the above. Rude people may well occupy influential positions for intermittent periods, but nobody enjoys working with them and, over time, the system spits them out. If you work on your own, there is absolutely no point in dealing with people of this type. They ruin your life and they do not deserve your contribution. Avoid them like the plague.

### ▶ They never answer their landline

This may not be the end of the road. Most landlines contain a message that mentions the name of a colleague or a mobile number. This gives you another way in. Depending on the nature of the business and the person you are calling, you may feel that it is appropriate to call their mobile, or speak to the colleague in question. Your decision here may be aided by looking at their website to see whether their mobile numbers feature. If they do, you have clearance to proceed.

**Try it now:** Cold calling?

Every time you make a call, you learn something. Their colleague's name, their mobile number, their daily pattern. It's all useful information. When you get through, you might even enjoy it. You might think it's cold, but the other person might not. So take the plunge and surprise yourself.

# Admit that the phone will never ring unless you market yourself

Many people who set up on their own make the mistake of thinking that the phone will ring and provide them with work in the same way that it did when they were employed in a company. It doesn't. In fact, on some days, it doesn't ring at all. One or two extremely blessed individuals come out of corporate life and seem to have a charmed flow of ready-made work without appearing to have to market themselves. But one thing is for sure: it never lasts. In year two or three, these people are left adrift as that source of business fades.

Besides which, you may not even have a contact base from a former life. In this case, you need to market yourself from the outset, to a fairly broad audience. The first stepping stone in this process is admitting that the phone is unlikely to ring unless you make it do so. In other words, you need to create the momentum that makes people want to call you back, whether that is today or at some point in the future when they have a need for your product or service.

This is a very simple piece of logic. If you don't ask the guy out, he won't even know you are interested. If you don't call and express an interest, then potential customers won't consider you.

# If you make 100 calls, you will get 40 meetings, and three jobs

The precise figures may vary depending on the nature of your business, but the essence of the equation never does. Take a moment to think about this. It stands to reason that you must generate a critical mass of interest in what you have to offer. The mathematics of it has nothing to do with the quality of you, your product or service, or your customer base. If you jot down all the possible reasons why someone does not want to do business with you this week, you will soon see how circumstances are more likely to stop work happening than to start it.

Start with these reasons why people will have no need for your services this week, and add your own:

▶ Holiday

▶ Illness

▶ Apathy

▶ Disorganization

▶ Budget change

▶ Colleague disagreeing

▶ Company politics

▶ A rival proposal

▶ Other priorities

▶ Haven't got round to it.

You could double the length of this list in less than a minute.

That's without even entertaining genuine, overriding, business considerations such as price, quality, distribution, over-supplied markets or product specification. Once you think about it, it's a miracle that anything ever gets done at all.

### ▶ Remember: 100 calls = 40 meetings = three jobs

This is why people keep talking about the 'pipeline' in a new business context. In truth, it is more helpful to see it as a funnel or hopper. The work appears to come sequentially in a linear way, but actually it only appears to be that way because, at any given moment, you have many contacts and proposals which, in all probability, will generate work at some point, but not necessarily now. It never happens all at once, and that is precisely why you need a regular flow of people who just might be interested in your offer in any given week or month.

When you run your own business, the moment you believe that you have a settled and steady customer base, everything may well be about to go wrong. Why? Because you will have failed to prime your next source of business to replace the business that you will inevitably lose soon, based purely on the law of averages. Some people claim that they fail to do this because they are too busy. This is a very poor excuse, particularly when you consider the huge irony of having too much time on your hands when you have lost a significant customer.

Perhaps another reason for not preparing is that you don't think it will happen to you because your quality is high and your relationship with your customers is good. That may well be true, but it has almost nothing to do with whether you will retain them or not. At some point, the law of averages will cause some factor you had not considered to jeopardize your business.

It may not be 'your fault', but it will certainly be 'your problem', so anticipate it and fix it before it is irretrievably broken.

### Unlock the facts: 100 calls = three jobs

This equation might be wrong, but the principle isn't. The more work you put in, the more you get out. So work out an appropriate ratio for the medium you are using. If the returns are too poor for the effort needed, then consider whether to use a different approach.

## Prepare your selling angles

Now let's get down to the business of what you are actually going to say on the phone. You've done the hard part: you've sat down with a list of people to call, researched all their numbers (see Chapter 2), and you've dialled. So what exactly are you going to say? You need to consider some selling angles:

► Who are you?

► What do you do?

- ► Why are you calling?

- ► What do you (or your business) offer?

- ► What has it got to do with them?

- ► What do you want to happen next?

- ► What happens if they are not there and someone else answers?

You need to work through all these possibilities before you call.

Don't dial and then panic. If you have considered all the angles beforehand, you won't be caught on the hop.

Never leave a message. If you do, you immediately cede control of the contact to the other person. This means that, the moment you call again, you are pestering.

# Don't use jargon to disguise what you do

So you have got through to the person you want to speak to. Stay calm. Remember that waffle and jargon are the last preserve of corporate behemoths. We all know that obscure phraseology is designed to confuse people so that it seems as though you need their services (and so that they can charge you more). But when you work on your own, the opposite is true. If they can't grasp what you do in one sentence, they won't bother to listen to the rest. Cut out the waffle and come straight to the point. If you are unfamiliar with the word 'obfuscation', look it up in the dictionary. It will say something like 'to make something unnecessarily difficult to understand'. This is the opposite of what you want to achieve.

Use clear, simple expressions to explain what you do and why you would like to do business with the potential client. Don't be vague about what you do – let them grasp it quickly and move the conversation on to the area that matters to you.

If you find this difficult, and you still sound vaguer than a vague thing, try some of these techniques:

- ► Pretend you are explaining it to your mother or father.

- ► Phrase it as though you were talking to your mate in the pub.

- Write it down and eliminate anything that sounds silly.

- Say it out loud and ask yourself whether you sound daft.

- Record it, listen back and decide if you would welcome such a phone call.

- Practise saying it in front of the mirror.

- Try it on the phone, then debrief yourself as to whether you sounded sensible – if not, draw up a new version.

But whatever you do, make sure you do all this before you call. It really is essential that you sound lucid and persuasive, and under no circumstances use a vital prospect as a guinea pig for a ham-fisted dry run that goes wrong. Get organized in advance and get it right.

**Remember this:** Don't use jargon

Disguising what you do behind impenetrable nonsense is the last bastion of the desperate. Become adept at describing what you do in less than 30 seconds. Get familiar with stating clearly and simply what your business does. If you waffle, they won't get it, and they certainly won't become a customer because they won't know what they are supposed to be buying.

# Tell them you are available

There is a tendency in modern business to create the impression that you are always frantically busy. This is completely inappropriate for someone who runs their own business. You need to strike the right balance. For a start, people soon detect whether you always claim to be very busy, and they probably won't believe it is always true. Moreover, if you really are so incredibly busy, how will you fit in the proposed work for them? Think about it. You need to convey the impression that you would like their business, but that it is not essential that you have it today. Desperation does not work. Confidence and calmness do.

Another side effect of always appearing to be frantically busy is that there is a distinct possibility that you will convey the impression that you are disorganized as well. This is a poor signal to be sending out. There is a good balance to be found in always making yourself available for potential business, but on your own terms and in your own time (within reason). Obviously you do not wish to come across as indifferent, but you should reserve the right to pace the flow of any new business advances to make sure that you deliver appropriately for your existing customers, because they pay the bills. When you are talking on the phone, make it clear that you are available to do the necessary work.

## Try selling the opposite of everyone else

It may seem fashionable to promote yourself or your business as specialist. Somehow people think it is more reassuring if they have a 'specialism', and to be fair there is some evidence that certain specialists are able to charge more for their services. Yet experienced business people can usually fix a whole range of issues, so it is important for you to think broadly. This is very likely to increase your opportunities, your income and the breadth of your work. This in turn will introduce greater variety to your work.

Of course, this suggestion presupposes that you are indeed capable of doing more than one type of thing. In theory it is possible that you genuinely cannot, but most people have more than one talent, and those who are capable of working on their own are certainly at the more enterprising end of the spectrum, and are usually used to fixing a range of problems. Give it some thought. Try portraying yourself as a generalist, not a specialist. You could get more work, and you will in all probability enjoy yourself more by venturing into new areas that you haven't tried before.

## Tell them it is simple (because you are experienced)

Tugging your beard and saying that something is really complicated does not inspire confidence and is as dismaying as a plumber staring at your boiler and declaring 'We'll never get the parts for this.' By all means appear thoughtful and reflective. Tell them that you have dealt with a similar issue before and that you know what to do – particularly if this is the first time you have spoken on the phone. A lot of work is commissioned not because the customers cannot do it themselves, but because they do not have the time. Consequently, it is often appropriate to tell them that they could certainly do the work themselves, but would it help if you took it off their 'Things to do' list for a certain price? At this point, speed and convenience may become more relevant than your precise skill set.

**Try it now: Tell them it's simple**

Don't bamboozle your customers. Tell them that you know how to fix the problem because you are experienced. That's what they want to hear, and why you can charge them for doing it. Your expertise does not have to be wrapped up in complication.

# Offer to solve their issue quickly

Doing something quickly doesn't mean that the work is bad quality or bad value. It may be precisely what the customer wants. As the old story goes, if a portrait costs £10,000, the painter is charging that for a lifetime's experience, regardless of whether he or she does the job in a day or a month. The speed with which you can do something has absolutely no bearing on the value. An experienced mechanic might diagnose and cure a problem in half an hour. An amateur might take all day, and may even do a poorer job of fixing it. The fast solution may actually be the higher quality one, assuming that the person in question knows exactly what they are doing.

This approach is also a pleasant counterpoint to suppliers who want to make a job last longer so that they can charge more. A good maxim for those who work on their own is:

*'Don't string it out in order to charge a higher price.'*

Offer to fix something quickly based on the assumption that you are experienced enough to know what you are doing, and organized enough to schedule it in efficiently and get on with it. If it is a business issue that needs resolving, offer to do it as a commando raid in a reasonably short space of time (you will be able to judge the appropriate timing based on your intimate knowledge of your sector). If you do the job well, you will have a satisfied client, and you will have been paid a good price for a sensible outlay of time. In short, neither party will have wasted any time.

## Be ready with examples of customers for whom you work

People love case histories, and when you catch them on the phone they don't usually have much time. They want easy anchor points on which to base their purchasing decision, just like references on a CV. They want to ask:

▶ Who else have you worked for?

▶ What did you do for them?

▶ Can I have some examples?

You need to anticipate these requests and, after a short while, you should be able to rattle these off effortlessly, even in your early days when you may actually be using examples from your previous corporate life. You do not always have to refer to something directly related to the task in hand, but you should become skilled at drawing on examples and making links between issues.

Customers do not always want people with direct experience of their field. Of course the narrow-minded ones might, but you wouldn't want them as customers anyway, now would you? Very often people in particular businesses have become too close to the issues that they encounter every day. This is something I call 'going native'. If they are smart enough to realize this, they will welcome a fresh perspective. That's where you come in. It is extremely likely that your skills are transferable and that they could benefit another business area if applied thoughtfully. So don't be sheepish about your skills – simply think broadly and suggest how your strengths could benefit the issue being discussed.

## Don't start discounting before you have even met

Don't start discounting on the phone. Your central maxim should be: 'Charge a premium price and do a great job'. State your rates clearly and without embarrassment. If they balk at the cost, say that you can discuss it when you meet and when you have better understood the nature of the possible work. Anyone who works on their own has examples of potential clients who have exclaimed 'How much?!', only to come back later with their tail between their legs having had a poor experience elsewhere with a cheaper alternative.

There are really only three variables at stake when a customer is considering whether to make a purchase: quality, price and timing. Put simply, the three questions are:

▶ Will it do the job?

▶ How much will it cost?

▶ When can I have it?

When you are negotiating, it is essential to remember that you can always have some flexibility on any two of the three variables, but never on all three. For example, you may be able to reduce the price if you are given a longer time. You may be able to do it quicker if you can charge more. And no one will ever admit to wanting low quality, but things can be short-circuited.

A good way to remember this negotiating stance is to try starting every sentence with the word 'if'. This ensures that you interrelate all the variables so that you never give all three away and end up in a pickle. For example, 'If I have to deliver it by Friday, the price will have to increase'; 'If you need the price to reduce, I will need longer to do the job.'

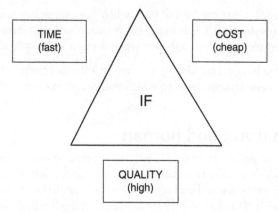

TIME
(fast)

COST
(cheap)

IF

QUALITY
(high)

**Figure 5.1** The 'if' triangle.

**Unlock the facts: Don't start discounting**

Some people discount even before they have met the customer. Don't do this. Explain what you do and what it costs. If they need what you have to offer, they might be perfectly happy with your full (non-discounted) price. If they propose a reduction you can always have a fallback position.

# Have a system for noting your calls

Keep a full list of all your contacts and have a system for contacting them – use the contact list and new business hit list that we looked at in Chapter 2. Keep them right up to date. Choose an appropriate contact frequency for your business that does not represent pestering. By all means note some detail about what was said if you think you might forget, but don't clutter the list with irrelevant stuff that might impede your next call. Staying organized in this area says volumes about your reliability and efficiency.

▶ The appropriate timing of your call says that you are diligent but not desperate or aggressive.

▶ The fact that you know when you last spoke shows that you are on the ball.

▶ The fact that you did call back when you said you would means that you are thoroughly organized and are therefore likely to be similarly efficient when doing a job for the client.

▶ If you have a new idea or have noted a development in their business circumstances to which you can refer, even better.

## Be natural and human

One final point when you are looking for new business, and particularly if you are talking to someone for the first time on the phone: be natural and remain true to your character. Keep your pride. Don't apologize for calling, and don't talk down what you have to offer. There is every chance that they will find your call helpful and interesting, and you'll never know unless you ask.

Remember one of the critical principles of running your own business: 'Only do business with people you like.' If they don't want to use you, it doesn't really matter. If they won't talk to you, it doesn't matter. Not everybody works with everyone else, and you will derive far more job satisfaction from working with people whose company you enjoy and who genuinely appreciate your contribution. In fact, many people leave larger companies precisely because they cannot find these qualities in their work. Therefore, there's not much point in working on your own if you simply end up replicating all the aspects of your previous working life that you were trying to change.

All you need is enough work to keep you stimulated and solvent. No adverse response is personal – it's just business. If it's not happening with a particular prospect, let it go, and keep your self-esteem intact. On the other hand, you will be jubilant when you have completed a successful call that has given you work. Then you will definitely know that you have tamed the telephone.

The ten golden rules of unsolicited calling*

1 Type out a list of people to call.

2 Print it out. If it's on the screen you won't do it.

3 Always print the phone number by the name. If you don't, you won't make the call.

4 Use a red pen to tick off your calls.

5 Never leave a message. If you do, you immediately cede control of the contact to the other person. This means that, the moment you call again, you are pestering.

6 If they are not there but someone else answers, ask for a good time to catch them, make a note, and call back. Do not be tempted to leave your name.

7 If you get voicemail, write down their mobile number and call them, or note any other information on the message and use it if appropriate.

8 When you do get through, make it sound as though it's the first time you've tried, even if it has taken weeks.

9 Make sure you can sell what you do in one sentence. Become adept at describing what you do rapidly and succinctly.

10 Always be cheerful and positive.

*Notice I have chosen not to call it 'cold calling'. It is your job to make it warm, and the client may well welcome your call, so think positive.

## Focus points

✱ Don't call it 'cold calling'.
✱ Admit that the phone will never ring unless you market yourself.
✱ Understand that 100 calls will get 40 meetings and three jobs.
✱ Prepare your selling angles.
✱ Do not use jargon to disguise what you do.
✱ Tell them you are available.
✱ Try selling the opposite of everyone else.
✱ Tell them it is simple (because you are experienced).
✱ Don't start discounting before you have even met.
✱ Have a system for noting your calls.

# 6

# Understanding time

In this chapter you will learn:

- ▶ *How everyone views time differently*
- ▶ *The two golden rules of time*
- ▶ *The six-month time lag*
- ▶ *How corporate time moves slower than normal time*
- ▶ *The Priority Matrix*

Now we are going to look at the concept of time. If it sounds like a heavy subject, don't worry. We won't be investigating the speed of light or debating the pros and cons of the space–time continuum. Although, so many of us rush around that it's not a bad thing to pause and reflect for a moment or two. Have you ever asked yourself what time is for?

Time passes whether we like it or not. How we measure the passage of time is one thing. How we describe it in universally acknowledged ways in order to be reasonably organized is another. Presumably that's why someone invented the calendar – in order for us all to know roughly where we are, or at least where we are supposed to be, at any given point. Perhaps one of the best definitions is that time was invented by humans to stop everything happening at once.

However, we need to answer this simple question:

> *What has time got to do with business?*

The answer, as you might expect, is: absolutely everything. We have already established that there are really only three things that matter when you are delivering something for a customer, which are:

▶ Will it do the job?

▶ How much will it cost?

▶ When can I have it?

There it is loud and clear in the third point: how quickly can you meet the client's request? If you fail to understand how time affects your business, then the basis of most of your plans and all your personal expectations are likely to be wrong. This is vital to what you do all day because, although plenty of things will happen eventually, they may all come far too late for you to pay the bills. Sounds over-dramatic? Let's investigate.

# Everyone views time differently

There are many dimensions to this assertion. Some of them make good sense. Others are a little more abstract. Yet they all have a direct effect on your ability to run a successful going concern, so let's consider a few of them.

First, as the person running the business, you will want to see progress and presumably some return on your effort and investment reasonably quickly, even if you are a very patient person. This desire has nothing to do with your customers whatsoever, and you need to be very careful that your agenda doesn't get in the way of your running a good operation or providing a decent service.

Think more about this. No single customer has the overview on your business that you do. You know the whole picture. You have a highly tuned knowledge of how much work you have, what the cash flow is, whether you can cope with the workload or not, and a million other details. Anyone else you speak to has no idea of any of this. Therefore, you need to judge very carefully whether the speed with which you want to progress something is suitable for your customer. If it is not, then they will at worst sense your desperation or at best think you are hasty or strangely frantic.

Second, there are often customers who do actually want things done in a hurry. This may or may not be appropriate to the nature of your business or your circumstances at any given time. If what you provide takes time and consideration to produce, then you need to reconcile such impatient requests with your personal and business standards.

Review your timing needs in relation to the possible outcomes that may occur if you hurry a job through. Here are some examples:

► In your rush to please someone at short notice, are you compromising on quality in a way that will come back to sully your reputation later?

► If you deliver at breakneck speed once, will they assume next time that this is the norm and ask for every job to be completed on that sort of timetable?

► By accepting a rush job, will you be displacing or inconveniencing an existing customer who always gives you sensible deadlines?

You need to consider these types of questions carefully and make sure that you do not create a noose for your own neck by establishing precedents that will be unhelpful later.

Third, bear in mind that, in many instances, something that takes longer to do or produce has a much higher perceived value. If a customer thinks that you have 'knocked something up quickly', then why should they wish to pay a higher price for it? Without being cynical, there are plenty of businesses in which it is preferable to take a little longer over something intentionally in order to emphasize the expertise that went into it. This observation is not intended to endorse the hoodwinking of customers by lying about how long something takes to do. It is, however, true that we live in an on-demand world, and the spirit of 'I want it now' can ruin your business if you give in too often. Make sure that, whenever humanly possible, you only accept appropriate deadlines for what you are being asked to do. The modern phenomenon of being time-poor is explored in detail in *Tick Achieve*, another of my books.

When you run your own business, there are two golden rules that are essential to your understanding of how time can affect your business:

### The two golden rules of time

1 Everything you do will involve a six-month time lag.
2 Corporate time moves slower than normal time.

Let's examine what these assertions mean.

### Remember this: Different views of time

Just because you want to get something done today doesn't mean that someone else does. The chances of your desires overlapping with someone else's are very low. Your version of fast or slow may not be theirs. So take a moment to work out whether you are being realistic.

# Everything you do will involve a six-month time lag

Six months is an indicative round figure designed to illustrate a point. Of course it might not be six months in your line of work. It doesn't really matter what the precise figure is. What does matter is that, when you have decided upon a plan, nothing ever happens as quickly as you expect (unless it is something that you did not plan, in which case it may happen very quickly and unexpectedly).

Here is a hypothetical chain of events that describes an average job in a service business, from the moment you begin the run-up to it, to the day on which you complete it, and get paid.

### GETTING THROUGH

If you call a prospective customer today, it will probably take two weeks to get through, assuming that the person you need to contact is unavailable at the precise moment that you happen to want them to be in. We discussed in Chapter 5 the many possible reasons for this, and consequently it is reasonable to assume that you will not initiate your idea on the very first day that you think of it.

### PLANNING THE MEETING

When you do eventually get through on the phone, the prospective client is very unlikely to be able to meet with you immediately to discuss what you have in mind. Let's say that they might be able to see you in three weeks.

### ACTUALLY MEETING

Most meetings are moved at least once before they occur. The chances of this happening to you are high, although the number of postponements may be related to the nature of your business. Remember that, until you are officially engaged to work for someone, you remain peripheral to the action. You will only become essential when you have been signed up, at which point you will probably be hugely in demand. The average is three postponements before the meeting actually takes place. That's another three weeks.

### TIME FOR THEM TO CONSIDER

After you have met, there will always be some sort of delay. Most customers need time to consider things. They have lots to do other than deal with what you have to offer. They probably have colleagues to talk to about you, and they may have competitors whose proposals they can compare with yours. After some deliberation, even if there genuinely is work to be had from that potential customer, it could easily take six weeks to come through.

## DOING THE WORK

Once commissioned, it may only take you a week to do the work, and of course this depends completely on what you do for a living. Nevertheless, regardless of your speed in delivering the goods, there will be customer comments, changes of mind and approval delays that will probably take another three weeks.

## SENDING THE BILL OUT

Let's be generous and say that you will be able to bill the job one week after you have finished it. This assumes that you have a sufficiently efficient system of sending out invoices every week, and that there is no uncertainty about invoicing immediately after a job is finished. (There are always touchy moments for those who work on their own when the bill has been sent but the customer doesn't accept that the job is finished because they feel there is still something left to tidy up.)

## GETTING PAID

It will most likely take them a minimum of six weeks to pay. Payment times vary hugely. Some retail and product-based transactions are settled on the spot. Some service projects are paid for within ten days, but these are the exception. At the other end of the scale, some companies take more than 100 days to pay up. Some even have a deliberate policy of refusing to do so for 90 days. That's three months, which to the person that works on their own can be an unmitigated disaster for cash flow.

Without going into a moral debate about how quickly people should be paid, you can now see that the combined effect of all these stages is likely to be around 24 weeks.

That's six months or, to be absolutely clear about this, half a year.

## How the six-month time lag works

Getting through to a prospective customer 2 weeks

Delay before you can meet 3 weeks

Rescheduling of meeting two or three times 3 weeks

Time for them to consider your proposal 6 weeks

Doing the job 3 weeks

Sending the bill out 1 week

Time taken for you to be paid 6 weeks

Total time 24 weeks

*24 weeks = six months = half a year*

Dramatic overstatement or business reality? Unfortunately, it is reality. You need to accept this fact quickly if you are to be a success on your own. This type of sequence is true to the majority of jobs – if you initiate something today, it is likely that the cheque will hit your doormat in about half a year. Once you have acknowledged this, you can reschedule your business plan, work out a much more realistic cash flow, and understand better the cycle of effort that you need to put in to get the work you need, when you need it.

This common-sense approach to accounting projections will stand you in much better stead than plugging in a mathematical formula from some accounting software or a bank's small business service. Be brutally honest with yourself and plan for the worst so that you will not be caught out.

We have already discussed how those who work on their own often fail to develop new business opportunities because they are supposedly too busy servicing existing business. Yet this six-month time lag equation demonstrates how short-sighted that approach is. By the time you are experiencing a lull in your current work, it could take half a year to reap the benefit of any renewed business effort. Unless you have a phenomenal stockpile of cash, this could prove fatal to your business. Therefore, without jeopardizing the quality of what you are currently up to, it is essential that you devote some time every month to developing new business possibilities.

**Unlock the facts:** The six-month time lag

Have an idea now, and it will take some time to come to fruition. Win a job today, and it will take time to complete. Send a bill and when will you get the money? That job, or the payment, may not occur until next year. Factor this in to your calculations.

## Corporate time moves slower than normal time

Has the author lost his bearings here? Surely we all work to internationally recognized standards of what time is, and we have all adhered to them for centuries? Whilst not disputing the accuracy of Greenwich Mean Time for one second (if you'll excuse the pun), it really is true that one person's perception of the passage of time can be completely different to another's. Think about how many times you have heard people say:

*'I can't believe it's Friday already.'*

*'This week has just flown by.'*

*'I don't know where the month went.'*

*'I can't believe it's Christmas so soon.'*

Some would probably argue that there is only a finite amount of time in the world, and that if busy people haven't got enough, idle people must have too much. Certainly, if you haven't got much to do, time drags. If you are busy, it rushes by. You really do need to take this into account when you are dealing with customers and prospects that are moving at a different pace to your personal desires. This is not the same point as the six-month time lag that we have just looked at.

Corporate time is different from personal time for many reasons. The main one is that working in an office involves doing all sorts of things that you would not ordinarily choose to do. Sitting in meetings is a particular culprit. Most meetings are attended by too many people who would probably rather be doing something else. In some extreme cases, people working for companies can spend as much as four days a week in meetings. This prevents them from doing the things that all the time spent in the meetings already committed them to do, and it makes them wonder where the week went.

It is also very much in the interests of someone working for a company to appear busy, regardless of whether they really are. In a company, the work expands to fit the time available to do it, in which case it is very rare for someone to claim that they have very little to do. Thus, corporate time really can be slower than normal time. This means that you need to re-calibrate your timing plans and expectations when working with larger companies.

**Remember this:** Corporate time v normal time

Companies are slower than individuals. It's as simple as that. The sole trader may well be busy, but probably in a more effective way. Companies generate processes, meetings and thousands of distractions that slow everything down. Bear this in mind when dealing with them.

## One day of personal time equals two weeks of corporate time

For anyone who runs their own business, the New Equation of Time is:

*'One day of personal time equals two weeks of corporate time.'*

This equation has been developed by the author over fifteen years and over six hundred jobs. Here are some guidelines based on this discovery in order to help you to understand how to deal with larger companies:

▶ You need to multiply every anticipated timing by a factor of ten working days in order to get a better flavour of how long it might really take.

- ▶ When they say that there will be a decision tomorrow, it means in a fortnight at the earliest.

- ▶ This phenomenon works the other way round – if you take a month off, it is the equivalent of a customer taking two working days off. No one will notice, let alone care. You should build this holiday into your business plan at the beginning of the year and adjust the income and anticipated work around it.

The moral of this discovery for those who run their own business is brutally simple:

> *'Whatever you plan to do, start now.'*

**Unlock the facts: 1 personal day = 2 corporate weeks**

One day of personal time equals two weeks of corporate time. When a company says that they will respond tomorrow, they mean in two weeks. Or never. They don't always mean to be mean, they just get distracted easily. Until it's urgent for them, and then they panic.

# Whatever you plan to do, start now

Prevarication is one of the greatest enemies of anyone who works on their own. Never put off something that needs doing, and never deny the truth. Take it on the chin and get it done. If you delay something, it will simply be there staring you in the face tomorrow. And the day after. And the day after that.

We can categorically state that the spirit of 'Maybe tomorrow' or 'Mañana mañana' has no place whatsoever in the lexicon of anyone who works on their own. If this is your natural tendency, either you should abandon your plans to run your own business now, or you will already have battled really hard and succeeded in overcoming it.

Adopt the 'Think Do' principle. If you are not a particularly organized person, at the very least you need to take on some of the trappings of someone who is, otherwise you won't be very effective on your own. Draw yourself a Priority Matrix with two axes based on urgent/not urgent, and important/not important. Now fill in your jobs to do.

► If it is urgent and important, do it now

► If it is urgent but not important, delegate it if you can (obviously this may be difficult because you work on your own, but you never know), or do it quickly first to get it out of the way

► If it is important but not urgent, think about what you need to do and plan when you are going to do it

► If it is neither important nor urgent, then why on earth are you doing it?

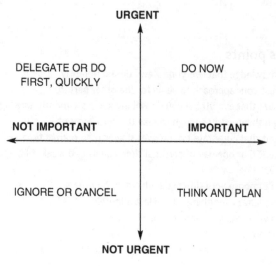

**Figure 6.1** Priority Matrix.

Regardless of the method by which you manage to get organized, organization definitely needs to become one of your strengths. Keep reminding yourself that if it needs to be done, then it has to be done by you. The task won't go away, and it will usually get worse the longer you leave it. The passage of time will trip you up in the end, unless you stick to the golden rule:

*'Whatever you plan to do, start now.'*

Time is a big issue, but if you stick to the five principles covered in this chapter, then you will be that much closer to understanding how different people view it, and how understanding this can really help to increase your chances of being a success.

### Try it now: Start now

'How do I get to Dublin?'

'If I were you, I wouldn't start from here.'

Everything has to start some time, so why not now? Whatever you plan to do, start now.

### Focus points

✳ Acknowledge that everyone views time differently.

✳ Adjust your approach to allow for the other person.

✳ Realize that everything you do will involve a six-month time lag.

✳ Begin things early enough to take this into account.

✳ Admit that corporate time moves slower than normal time.

✳ Accept that one day of personal time equals two weeks of corporate time.

✳ Don't impose your timescale arbitrarily on others.

✳ Don't leave everything till the last minute.

✳ Plan whatever you want to do.

✳ Start now.

# 7

# How to conduct yourself

In this chapter you will learn:

- ▶ *How to create a 'company culture' when you run your own business*
- ▶ *How to motivate yourself*
- ▶ *What to do and what not to do*
- ▶ *Why you should only do business with people you like*
- ▶ *Why talking to yourself is a good thing*

We have covered many of the emotional and practical aspects of how to run your own business. There is another utterly essential element that books cannot really teach you, but which requires careful attention nonetheless. It is not tangible. You can't buy it. You can't quantify or measure it. You may be able to acquire a few of the skills that allow you to believe that you have got 'it' about right, although you will never know for sure. So what is this elusive quality? It is how to conduct yourself.

When you work for yourself, the way that you come across is absolutely paramount. Within minutes, seconds even, you can convey completely the wrong impression. Your manners, your dress, your attitude – they all count for a great deal. They can lose the interest or respect of your potential customer in an instant. When you launch your own business, you owe it to yourself to consider very carefully what sort of image you wish to convey.

## You are the company culture

You need to confront the fact that, when you work on your own, you are the company culture. There are no hazy mission statements to fall back on, no Human Resources department, and no glossy brochure to cover up for shoddy behaviour. You need to behave as you would like others to behave. What does that mean? Well, disregarding personal style for a moment, there are some basic principles of good conduct to which you should adhere. For example:

► Be polite

► Be realistic

► Turn up on time

► Return calls when you say you will

► Pay your bills immediately

► Over-deliver if you wish, but never under-deliver.

You can create your own list of this type based on your personal preferences and the nature of your business. Over time, you will undoubtedly receive back as much good behaviour as you dish out. You will gain a reputation for high standards, integrity and honesty. Repeat business will follow.

Or, put another way, if you are small-minded, you will lose good customers and attract those who are also small-minded and unreliable. At an early stage, map out what you believe to be the important parts of how to conduct your business, and use that as a blueprint to determine how you should conduct yourself, and in turn what you expect and desire of others. This will stand you in good stead if you have to confront a dilemma about whether to decline some business, or if you have to take the harsh decision to inform an existing customer that you will no longer work with them. Making such a fundamental decision on the spot often comes across as impetuousness or impatience, but if you have thought through your principles carefully, you can state calmly and clearly that their way of doing things does not tally with yours. That's your right as someone who works on their own.

**Remember this:** You are the company culture

If you behave well, then your company will be well regarded. And vice versa. If you come across as an idiot, disorganized, untrustworthy, or any other negative characteristic, then so will your company. So keep an eye on how you conduct yourself and make sure it tallies with how you wish your company to be perceived.

# Only do business with people that you like

This is quite a tricky area but it really is worth spending the time to work out how you feel about your business relationships. Naturally, if you work in a service business or run a retail outlet you can't vet everybody with whom you have a transaction. But you can choose the nature of your suppliers and associates. And as you develop your own personal style, you will become better at working out what other people are like to deal with. Eventually, you should be in a position whereby it is you who chooses to do business with somebody, not the other way round.

Why is this important? Because ultimately if you do not enjoy the company of the people with whom you have to interact, you will effectively have engineered a state of affairs in which you don't like what you do. This is a disaster for anyone who runs their own business. Indeed, the whole point of working on your own is to design a set-up that suits your particular style. Of course, sometimes it takes a while for someone to show their true colours, and there will be times when somebody you really like lets you down.

Unfortunately, there is nothing you can do about this, and it is undoubtedly true that any disappointments will be felt harder by you as an individual than by companies in the collective sense. However, in the long run, your judgement will improve with experience, and your goal should be only to do business with the people that you like.

## Subsume your ego

There is a huge difference between having a particular personal style and having a big ego. Personal style is distinctive, desirable and an important element of why people choose to do business with you. Ego is destructive, selfish and impedes business relationships. If you want to be a success, and you have a big ego, you need to have a personal truth session and bury it. This is not so that you become an automaton with no character, but so that your skills and qualities can come to the fore and be seen to be of value by potential customers without your ego detracting from them. If you are showboating all the time, this is unlikely to be the case.

It often helps if you let your customers believe or claim that many of your ideas are theirs. You will get more repeat business. If you make someone look good, they will be eternally grateful. This is not sycophancy. When you hear that someone has 'bought into' one of your ideas, it means they have joined in and helped to convince themselves of the value of it. This is outstanding selling, and cannot happen if you keep banging on about how it was 'my idea'.

Another way of reconciling this with your ego is to remember that, once a client has paid you for your work, it is actually theirs. In the case of tangible products, this is obviously self-evident. But in the grey area of ideas and advice, even the 'copyright' of your recommendations becomes your clients' property, assuming that you have negotiated an appropriate price and taken intellectual property issues into account. It should in fact be a genuine piece of flattery if a client chooses to champion your work and goes so far as to claim it as their own.

# Do not distinguish between nice and nasty things to do

What a strange idea! It is human nature to say 'I love doing x' and 'I hate doing y'. Sadly, now that you are your own boss, you need to stop making the distinction between the two. Why? Because it was your decision to go it alone, and whatever needs doing has to be done and is ultimately entirely for your own personal benefit. Even if the task is working out how much tax to pay, it is worth doing well because if you don't, you will be the one to lose out.

It is also inaccurate to presuppose that something you expect to be nasty will actually turn out to be so. In reality, the outcome of a situation that you are anxious about is frequently the opposite of what you expect it to be. This may sound false but it is actually true. For instance, can you imagine how you might have a better meeting firing someone than giving them a pay rise? No? Have a look at these two examples.

▶ **Proof that nasty things can turn out to be nice**

*Employer*: I'm very sorry but after a lot of discussion and anxiety I'm afraid we can't keep you in this job any longer.

*Employee*: I can't say I'm surprised. I haven't been coping very well and I haven't been happy. I was thinking of going travelling instead.

▶ **Proof that nice things can turn out to be nasty**

*Employer*: I am pleased to tell you that we have agreed a £3,000 pay rise for you.

*Employee*: I'm really disappointed. I was expecting a minimum of £5,000.

So you see, that supposedly nasty cold call looming on your checklist might well be the very thing that makes you most happy this month. Go on. Get to it.

**Remember this:** Nice or nasty?

Chances are, if you try to guess the outcome of something, you'll be wrong as often as you are right. So stop second-guessing everything and get stuck in. If in doubt, do the worst first and get it over with. All the tasks need to be done, so don't distinguish between nice and nasty things to do – just get on with it.

## Talk to yourself

Talking to yourself is not a sign of madness. It is actually an extremely helpful way for someone who works on their own to clarify things when no one else is around. Saying things out loud is a highly constructive thing to do. Go on, say it out loud now. You can eliminate all manner of nonsense from letters if you take the trouble to read them out loud. Frequently, they sound ludicrous when you read them back. You know the sort of thing: 'Please do not hesitate to contact myself …' You would never speak like that, so don't write that way either.

Talking out loud also cures twaddle and jargon on presentation charts, waffle in marketing material, and spouting garbage on the telephone. If you practise your telephone pitch out loud and conclude that you sound like a twit, then that is clearly time well spent.

Another benefit of talking to yourself is that at least you are guaranteed a decent conversation and, although you may disagree with yourself, at least you won't have a flaming row! Despite what the amateur psychologists say, it's healthy, it's amusing, and for those of you poor people who miss the office, it provides a bit of banter about the place as well.

## Remind yourself of all the positive things you have done

This is not a piece of self-delusion therapy. It is simply the knack of staying positive. All self-employed people suffer from some form of self-doubt. You don't have colleagues congratulating you on a job well done, so you need to generate your own humble form of self-congratulation. Think about it. No one else is going to bother, so you need to find a private way to celebrate your successes and keep your confidence levels up.

Consider these ideas for reminding yourself that you are actually pretty good at what you do and that you deserve a pat on the back:

▶ Write down your income.

▶ Write down your profit.

▶ Say out loud: 'I am still in business.'

▶ Choose which recent business transaction was your favourite.

▶ Ask a customer if they will write a reference for you.

▶ Ask your partner or a friend if they think you are any good at what you do.

▶ Invent an ingenious plan for the near future.

▶ Calculate whether you can afford a holiday soon.

▶ Book a holiday.

▶ If you have rivals, consider whether they are doing as well as you.

Remember this straightforward maxim:

*'Everything you achieve, you have done yourself.'*

# Never moan

Moaning is one of the most unattractive features of any personality. Whose company would you prefer? Someone with a positive, optimistic outlook or someone who spends the whole time bellyaching about things that aren't going well? Moaning is unacceptable for anyone who works on their own. Why? Because it is actually an admission of failure. If you don't agree, here is a simple translation of a moaner's conversation to illustrate the point:

> *Bloke in pub: 'Business is really tough at the moment and things aren't going very well.'*

There are two possible translations of this remark:

> *'I am not talented enough to get the work I want.'*

or:

> *'I am too lazy to get the work I need.'*

This is not an exaggeration. If you run your own business, then your fortunes are entirely in your hands. You can invoke as many higher powers as you like, blame macro-economic conditions and invent reams of blether about precisely why you don't have enough work at the moment. None of this smokescreen will disguise the fact that you haven't had the wit or the determination to go and get it. This is not some assertion cooked up by a motivation guru or a sales zealot. It is cold, hard logic. So type it up and stick it on the wall: *No moaning.*

There is one other essential part of the 'No moaning' credo. Never be tempted to join in with a customer who is moaning. You can sympathize briefly, but then it is your job to suggest ways in which you can make it better, otherwise these dreadful people will rapidly turn you into a moaner too.

### Remember this: Never moan

Some you win, some you lose. Get over it. Work is called work because it involves effort. You get paid for what you put in. Remind yourself of this regularly and, if you ever catch yourself having a moan, nip it in the bud early. Never moan in front of customers. Nobody is interested.

## Never drink during the day

Does this point really need clarification? Then go back and work for a company. This is a no-brainer. The same goes for drugs and anything else that has the capacity to turn you into a blithering idiot during work hours. Save it for the weekend! If you ever receive a call from a customer in the afternoon and you are less than compos mentis, your reputation will be on the slide immediately. 'I wouldn't use him, he's a bit of a drinker' is not how you would wish to be described around town. If you really do have to have a near-compulsory jolly with a customer one day, then turn your mobile off and return any calls when you are sober, saying that unfortunately you were in an all-day meeting or out of town. Never get involved in important business when you are in danger of talking rubbish.

## Never watch daytime TV

As with drinking, watching daytime TV is the rapid road to Loserville. What makes this so obvious?

▶ You should be working.

▶ You won't learn anything.

▶ After a short while, your IQ will probably fall.

If you disagree with this and insist on watching this drivel, then you only have two possible courses of action:

1 Reduce the quality of your work from now on to reflect your new low-level intellect.

2 Lower your prices immediately to reflect your diminished aspirations.

## Never finish a day before deciding what to do the next morning

This simple little discipline works incredibly well. It is outstandingly easy to do, and is the best ever way of ensuring a good night's sleep. Simply write down what you have to do the next day and, if appropriate, allocate the necessary time for it. Now you can relax. There are many subsidiary benefits to this approach. First, it is impossible to forget to do something because it is written down. Second, you come across as totally on the ball because you genuinely do know what you are doing the next day. And third, you don't have to worry about the tasks for the next day so you can go and have that drink after all.

# Never do anything unless you know why you are doing it

How blindingly obvious is this statement? It would be a good principle for all businesspeople to abide by. Actually, it applies to anything you ever do in your whole life. This is so profoundly irrefutable that it is worth stating again:

> 'Never do anything unless you know why you are doing it.'

It stands to reason. Think carefully about what you are doing and why you are doing it. Your time is your potential money. If you are doing something unnecessary, then for every minute you do so, you are shooting yourself in the foot. Only do the things that matter. Your time is too precious to approach it any other way.

### Unlock the facts: Why am I doing that?

You'd be amazed how many people do things without really knowing why. Don't let it be you. Take a few moments to work out whether the thing you are about to do will achieve the result you desire. If you conclude that it won't, then don't do it. Never do anything unless you know why you are doing it.

# Have reserve plans for every day

When you start out working on your own, you may well quite naïvely assume that the shape of tomorrow will be exactly as it is written in your personal organizer. Nothing could be further from the truth! Just when you have put a suit on, on a day when you think you have three meetings, they may have all been cancelled by 9.30 a.m. If that does happen, it is not acceptable to sit around and do nothing on the grounds that everything has changed. In fact, you should assume every day that everything will change.

Being incapable of adapting rapidly is a big warning sign for anyone who works on their own. Expressing dismay that everything has changed at short notice conveys the impression that it is easy to catch you on the hop and that you are a bit of a plodder. Life's a mess – roll with it and enjoy the ride!

You need Plans B, C and so on that you can engage immediately when all the other activities fall away. The trick to avoid disappointment is to work out that this *will* happen *before* it happens. Then when it does, which it undoubtedly will, instead of being aghast at this extraordinary development and going into a flat spin, you simply reach for your Plan B file. Let's have a look at what a Plan B might be, and relish the thought that the wonderful thing about Plan B is that Plan B is often more productive than Plan A.

## Remember that Plan B is often more productive than Plan A

Here are 12 examples of things that anyone can do to generate a Plan B.

1  As a matter of course, you should read all the trade press related to your business, and that which your potential customers read, plus anything else that stimulates you. Collect ideas and articles, and use them to generate initiatives and give you the basis for a speculative phone call or proposal.

2  If an ex-customer or colleague surfaces somewhere in a new job, call them immediately, and keep an eye out for information on the new market that they have entered. This is how you will extend your customer base beyond its current shape.

3  Have good data sources, become familiar with them and use them to generate ideas. In particular, remember that trends change all the time, so you cannot claim to be on top of developments if you don't check them regularly.

4  Read more books than your customers. Barely anyone in any industry has ever read what they are supposed to. If you have, you can help by introducing new ideas and by being the authority on a specific subject.

5 Collect interesting quotes that may help to liven up presentations or marketing materials. It is a tricky business looking for inspiration at the precise moment that you need it. The whole thing is much easier if you make a habit of collecting stimulating quotes all the time. Then when you need some inspiration, you can simply reach for your quotes file.

6 Look up a word in the dictionary every day to make yourself more erudite (look that one up if you need to). Obviously this is a matter of personal choice, but we only use a fraction of the words available in our language and it can become very dull. The beauty of working for yourself is that, if you want to look up a word on the spot, then you usually can. People in companies rarely want to admit to a colleague that they don't know the meaning of a word, let alone that they don't possess a dictionary.

**abrogate** *vb* to cancel an agreement

**baronial** *adj* acting like a powerful businessman

**chimera** *n* an unrealistic dream or idea

**diatribe** *n* a bitter critical attack

**egregious** *adj* shockingly bad

**fresco** *n* wall painting using watercolours on wet plaster

**garrulous** *adj* constantly chattering or talkative

**hubris** *n* pride or arrogance

**interpolate** *vb* to insert into a conversation or text

**jocund** *adj* cheerful or merry

**kaput** *adj* ruined or broken

**languorous** *adj* in a vague, dreamy state

**mollify** *vb* to make someone less angry

**necromancy** *n* sorcery or communication with the dead

**omnipotent** *n* all-powerful

**peripatetic** *adj* travelling from place to place

**quasi-** almost but not really

**riparian** *adj* on the bank of a river

**snig** *vb* to drag a felled log by a cable

**tremulous** *adj* trembling from fear or excitement

**utilitarian** *adj* useful rather than beautiful

**vapid** *adj* dull and uninteresting

**waspish** *adj* bad tempered or spiteful

**xerox** *n* photocopy

**yorker** *n* cricket ball bowled just under the bat

**zephyr** *n* a soft gentle breeze

*vb* = verb; *adj* = adjective; *n* = noun

7 Improve your grammar and phraseology so that you can express yourself better than your customers and competitors, obviously without turning into a pompous fool. In certain businesses, you can even sell this as a skill in its own right because all companies can improve how they communicate. The overall effect will be to reinforce the fact that you are good at what you do and can express yourself well.

8 Hobbies and projects are good to have at hand, so long as they do not take over your working life. They can provide an excellent counterbalance to work if you have a lot of intensive stuff to do over a sustained period, and customers will find your other talents interesting because they complement their perception that you are an enterprising person with plenty of ideas and energy.

9 More specifically, when you have achieved something extracurricular, make it part of your CV and sales patter. People are interested, and it adds a human dimension to the person behind the business skills that they are being offered.

10 Constantly rewrite your CV, redefining your skills again and again to reflect what you are best at, and what you enjoy

doing most, based on the new work you are doing. Don't forget that what you are best at and what you enjoy most are often strongly related. This is very much part of the joy of working on your own – you can dictate, within reason, the nature of the work that you choose to do, and mould it as you develop your understanding of yourself.

11  Regularly examine the shape of your business so that you can rattle off the facts to your clients. For example:

   a  How many clients did you have in year 1/2/3?

   b  How many jobs did you do in year 1/2/3?

   c  How much repeat business did you have in year 2?

12  Look at the bottom of your contact list and call everyone below the Pester Line.

If after all those suggestions you are still able to claim that you have no idea what to do with your time, you should definitely not be running your own business. And whether you agree with the ideas of how you should behave or not, you should definitely now be able to draw up your own rules of engagement, so that you are never unsure about how to conduct yourself. Once you do, you will have created your own 'company culture', and your potential customers will be left in no doubt as to what you stand for.

It is then up to your potential clients to decide whether your style suits them, and if you have conducted yourself well, then it is very likely that it will.

### Remember this: Plan B v Plan A

Don't get upset when Plan A doesn't happen. The good news is that Plan B is often more productive than Plan A. How fun is that? Don't call it fate or invoke a higher power. Just move on to the next thing. And don't forget Plans C, D, E and beyond...

## Focus points

- ✲ Acknowledge that you are the company culture.
- ✲ Subsume your ego.
- ✲ Do not distinguish between nice and nasty things to do.
- ✲ Remind yourself of all the positive things you have done.
- ✲ Never moan.
- ✲ Never drink during the day.
- ✲ Never watch daytime TV.
- ✲ Never finish a day before deciding what to do the next morning.
- ✲ Never do anything unless you know why you are doing it.
- ✲ Remember that Plan B is often more productive than Plan A.

# 8

# Meetings can be fun

In this chapter you will learn:

- ▶ *What to do when you secure a meeting*
- ▶ *What to do in meetings*
- ▶ *What to do after meetings*
- ▶ *How to ask what is on a client's mind and offer to fix it*
- ▶ *How to be more positive than everyone else all the time*

Meetings. The very word invokes feelings of dread in some people. Even people who appear to be very confident in any other situation can freeze up and behave strangely. Yet with the right approach, meetings do not have to be daunting at all. Actually, they can be great fun, so let's have a look at some of the techniques that can make this a possibility.

# When you secure a meeting, get organized straightaway

*'Efficiency is a sophisticated form of laziness.'*

Give this claim some careful thought. The more sorted you are, the less you need to panic. The better organized you are, the less time you will waste faffing about at the last minute in a state of disarray, and the more time you will have to enjoy yourself on your own terms. There is also a strong chance that the quality of what you produce will be higher, better considered and more fulfilling.

As soon as you have secured a meeting, take the time to work out exactly what you need in order to make it a success. This might include:

▶ Your CV

▶ Client list

▶ Case histories

▶ Examples of what you produce

▶ A list of ways in which you may be able to help

▶ A proposal or the outline of one

▶ Research or observations on their market and the issues they face

▶ Price list

▶ Terms of business.

If the need for these materials is fairly obvious, then immediately print them off and assemble them in a sensible way, with enough copies for everyone. How many times have you been to a meeting where people that have never been mentioned before turn up? You need to anticipate this and have spares of everything that matters so that you come across as professional and can address your ideas to the attendees who are going to have a direct bearing on the purchasing decision.

Now put your materials in a folder marked with the name of the people you are meeting and, if you need to, the date (but bear in mind that it will almost certainly change). If it needs more thought than that, either do the thinking now or write the preparation time in your personal organizer straightaway, always leaving plenty of time to do it before the day. This is particularly important because, if it does need more thought, it is highly likely that you will uncover more complicated issues when you do get round to reviewing it. If this is the case, then preparing moments before the meeting will be cutting it too fine.

The 'Think Do' principle will serve you well when running your own business. Apply this to your meeting preparation and to what you do after you have had the meeting and have agreed that there are things to be done. There is often quite a gap between a meeting being arranged and it actually taking place. This can cause problems because, if you don't get organized now, you may well forget the subtleties of what the meeting is truly about, or indeed, what you have *chosen* to make it about. This may sound odd, but many people just write 'meeting with x' in the diary and think no more about it until the day before. This is hopeless. The clever angles are usually all lurking in the original phone call, and the only way to capture these is to *do it now*.

The same is true after a meeting. All the details and nuances are fresh in your mind and, although some issues may certainly require longer consideration, the chances are that your first instincts about roughly what needs to be done in response to a particular issue are about right. Make those decisions now and prepare your response. Under no circumstances convince yourself that it's okay to ignore it all because the follow-up meeting or your official response isn't due for a couple of weeks. By then you will have forgotten some of the finer points, and your response will be poorer as a result. With this organized approach, you can never be caught out by a meeting, even in the very unlikely event that you have forgotten all about it until the last minute.

Another important activity related to this level of organizational discipline is to examine your personal organizer often, not only to survey that day's appointments, but to look ahead and anticipate your flow of work. Thinking ahead is your best ally in the tricky business of dealing with many things at once. The better you are at doing things now, the more freedom you will have to accept other speculative work as and when it crops up. It also reduces your worry levels because you know for sure that you really *are* prepared for something, no matter how far in the future it is, and now you can relax and get on with something else, be it work or pleasure.

# Get chronological

Put your files in the order in which the meetings are due so that, on any given morning, you can simply reach for the relevant folder and walk out of the door. As the meeting dates change, change the chronological order of your prepared files. This approach completely circumnavigates the sort of panic that usually precedes a meeting for which you have not prepared. Remember, now that you work on your own, it is *your* choice whether you wish to be prepared or not. You no longer have the excuse of blaming someone else or other external (and supposedly uncontrollable) factors – although as we have already established, these are not usually valid excuses anyway. Nor do you have so many other distractions, unless you deliberately choose to allow something else to get in your way.

There are, of course, those who claim that the last minute, student-style 'essay crisis' approach to preparation also works for them in business. This really doesn't make any sense at all and usually comes across as a pretty thin argument. Whilst it may be true that certain characters only pull their finger out and do the necessary work when they are under pressure and so forced to, this is a dreadful way to operate when you work for yourself. It gives you no time for reflection or improvement of your proposals; only one attempt at a given issue; and usually mistakes creep in, making you look unprofessional. It is far better to contemplate something in good time and be completely ready for the task at hand.

## Research everything thoroughly

Being well prepared wins you business and gains you customers. Do plenty of research so that you know what you are talking about and have some interesting lines of enquiry to pursue. Try some of the following:

▶ Investigate the company on the internet and via any other sources you can obtain.

▶ Critique these sources so that you have an opinion on how the company presents itself.

▶ Be inquisitive. Ask 'why?' several times in a row to work out why things are as they are.*

▶ Write down a list of issues that affect the potential customer.

▶ Find out as much as you can about the customer as an individual.

▶ Are there colleagues involved too?

▶ What are their issues and angles?

▶ Go to the meeting with lots of informed observations.

▶ Take a list of questions to stimulate conversation.

▶ Draw up a list of some ways in which you can help.

(*Another of my books, *So What?*, contains every question you'll ever need to solve business problems. It's all about asking enough of them until you solve the problem.)

## Give the client a list of ways in which you can help

Draw up a list of ways in which you think you can help the prospective client. This list is an absolute winner. No one can resist reading it for a start. The fact that you have made plenty of suggestions proves that you have plenty of ideas, and that you have been thinking about their business, which is always flattering because people always love talking about their own area. This level of enterprise and enthusiasm also means that it doesn't matter if you have made a couple of inaccurate assumptions, because they will be seen as forgivable in relation to your obvious keenness for the other matters in hand.

During the thousand or more meetings in which this approach has been tested, on average a minimum of two things on your list will be appropriate to the potential customer that day. Rest assured, that's two more than most speculative suppliers come up with. It is also a thoughtful and diligent thing to do because the ideas are specific to their business, and have the power to elevate you above the normal supplier who only brings along the standard materials that they clearly use for every other meeting.

What will set you apart is the degree to which you are inquisitive. Many people go into meetings simply trying to find a home for products or services that they already have, and then selling them as hard as possible. This approach has only limited success because it depends entirely on whether there is potential in the market for that sort of thing *at that precise moment*. With your more inquisitive approach, you will be suggesting ideas and asking questions. The opportunity lies in listening carefully to the answers, and adapting your skills to see if you can help at all. Chances are that you will be able to.

 **Try it now: How can I help?**

You've heard the question hundreds of times in retail outlets. You can also use it in meetings. Better still – write it down. Give them a list of ways in which you can help. This shows that you have thought about their issues in advance. It also offsets the possibility that the thing you thought was important wasn't, and vice versa.

## Include things that you *could* do, even if you have never done them

It is fine to stick to known territory when you are launching your business, but after a while you may find your work a little monotonous and so wish to broaden your scope. Alternatively, you may have reached the stage where the demand and income for your core offerings do not have enough value to sustain the income or margin that you desire. This broader approach of suggesting what you *could* do (rather than what you have always done before) could lead you into some very interesting areas and might serve you well.

It is certainly worth trying if you find that your standard list of suggestions is not generating enough work. This may mean that the way in which you are describing what you offer is not striking the right sort of chord, or that there is not enough of a market for it at the moment. If so, you could reinvigorate your business by broadening your offering.

Later on in your solo life, if you have become somewhat bored with the sameness of your work, the value of offering to do things you have never done before will be stimulating and re-energizing. If you do receive a favourable response to a proposal, you will enjoy the challenge of working out how to do it, and will probably learn new skills in the process. Don't be scared of this – you will never find yourself proposing something that is so far beyond your skill set that you genuinely could not cope with the new challenge of doing it.

## Ask what is on the client's mind at the moment and offer to fix it

Ask what is currently on the potential customer's checklist. Everyone has a checklist, and the average contains about 20 to 25 items. There is an approximate mathematical reason for this. If someone has very little to do (say, five things or fewer), there is little point in having a list because they can remember the items easily enough. On the other hand, if someone has so much to do that the number of tasks exceeds, say, 30, then they won't write down any more than that because the list will be too daunting. Human nature dictates that no one wants to stare at a seemingly endless list of things to do because it will be too depressing. So, even if there genuinely *are* more things to do than that, they certainly won't bother to write them down.

Therefore, the average list will have 20 or so things on it. This makes the author feel sufficiently busy and yet just about in control of what they are doing. The top three problems on it will probably be fixable by the owner of the list or by one of their colleagues. Anything that is below item number ten on their list of things to do, and is still there at the end of every week, is the sort of thing that you should offer to fix.

Everyone has them. After a while they can't even remember why the item was put on the list in the first place. Often they have been asked by a boss to do it and they can barely remember why. You can even ask them what they would regard as a fair price to remove it from the list, and decide if that represents a viable amount for your purposes. Few can resist the offer of having a troublesome item like this removed from their list, and don't forget that you can often negotiate the price after you have established the need.

### Unlock the facts: What's on your mind?

Asking open-ended questions can lead to great results. Let your potential customers identify their own needs. Ask what is on their mind at the moment and offer to fix it. This means that you will not be imposing something on them that they don't want or need, and it could lead you into some interesting new areas.

## Listen more than you talk

This shouldn't really need any explanation. The old adage goes that you have two ears and one mouth, and should use them in that proportion. Listening hard unlocks all manner of issues that will enable you to help with, comment on, rectify, debate and, above all, engage your potential customer. If possible, you should ask a simple question that requires only one answer. Then shut up and pay attention. An example of such a question might be:

> *'What is bothering you most at the moment?'*

Multiple questions don't work very well because it is rare that all the points are actually answered in the one response. An example of a bad question might be:

> *'Why is that an issue – I thought David had dealt with that last month and wasn't it supposed to be part of Project Pineapple anyway?'*

This gives the potential client every opportunity to choose not to answer the question or, even if they genuinely did intend to answer it, to become distracted by one of the subsidiary points and so not really get to the main one. This serves no purpose and is to your detriment because it significantly reduces the chance of you finding out anything useful. It is far better to ask about one thing, hear the reply, understand it, and then move on to the next one.

**Try it now: LISTEN, talk**

Listen more than you talk. The old adage of having two ears and one mouth, and using them in that proportion, is wise advice. Understanding how you can help comes from paying attention. So listen hard, otherwise you won't learn anything.

# Be more positive than everyone else in every meeting

People enjoy having meetings with positive, interesting people. This is not only true of business, but of any social encounter. The corollary of this is that no one enjoys meeting with a negative person. Consequently, it is essential that you can never be accused of being such a person.

Unfortunately, a lot of people have to do business with boring people who don't say what they mean and don't contribute anything positive. This needn't necessarily matter (provided you can retain your sense of humour in any given meeting) because by comparison you can only come across as more positive and alert than they are. Many people in business are simply 'killers' – those who constantly block ideas but never actually suggest any themselves. They bring everything down and even have the capacity to make *you* look bad by association if you do not have your wits about you. Do not let this happen. It is your job to remain enthusiastic (see Chapter 9, 'Staying sane and relentlessly enthusiastic'), because this will ensure that you are always a pleasure to have at meetings and are a constant source of helpful suggestions.

Now that you run your own business, you need never behave in a negative way. Go into meetings like a breath of fresh air, brimming with ideas. Enthusiasm is infectious. Many issues are tricky, but that doesn't mean that they have to be dealt with in a dull or negative way. Tackle the tough stuff head on, and come up with lots of ways of improving things. Customers love it, if only because it is often such a contrast to those who are happy to potter along and have a good old moan without suggesting anything positive. And of course the best compliment you can receive is when your customers always look forward to having meetings with you because of the difference you make in every encounter.

**Remember this: Be positive**

Ever been to a meeting and come out totally drained because everyone else was so negative? It's a horrible feeling, and not one that you want to transmit. Who wants to have a meeting with a boring, negative person? Nobody. So be more positive than everyone else in every meeting you attend.

# Never be late

Being late is just plain rude. In most cases, it is also totally avoidable and completely inexcusable. It doesn't take a genius to realize that if you have never been to the venue of a meeting before, you should allow extra time so that you have some leeway for heading to the wrong end of a very long street or underestimating the length of a journey. If you do turn up early, you can use the time to relax and run through what you plan to say once more. There's nothing wrong with saying that you had an idea on the way to the meeting. In fact, it proves that you are constantly thinking about the client's business issues.

A happy side effect of this approach is that, if it is *they* who are late, you will begin the meeting with something of a psychological upper hand. Stay calm and take it all in your stride. By comparison you will seem professional and prepared, which will imply that if they do end up engaging your services, you will be likely to deal with their work in the same orderly way.

Put another way, no one wants to do business with a breathless, shambolic person. This is an important point that is closely linked to the accuracy of your self-perception. You will have had occasions where you have been dismayed by someone else's business conduct, and we examined in Chapter 7 how you can work out how *you* should behave. Meeting etiquette is merely an extension of this philosophy, and you would never want to feel that you come across as poorly as any of those people in the past whom you feel have been a let down. So turn up on time.

**Remember this:** Never be late

What do we deduce about people who are late? Are they disorganized Rude? Too stupid to allow sufficient time for the journey? One way or another, your impression of them diminishes. So don't let that person be you. Being late is disrespectful, and suggests that you are incompetent.

# Be spontaneous and act naturally

If you are asked for a proposal, an opinion or a price, suggest one straightaway. This does not convey a hurried approach. Nor does it suggest that you make things up on the hoof. It only confirms your experience in dealing with things quickly and authoritatively.

Remember that you no longer have to consult with a colleague because you haven't got any. Sometimes it is actually worth pointing this fact out to the potential customer. A lot of people fall into the trap of saying, 'I'll have a think about that and get back to you.' Of course, if the problem is highly complex, you may want to retire gracefully to consider it further. But most of the time, in doing so you are simply introducing another barrier to the sales process, and creating another delay, which is quite unnecessary. Go on instinct!

Your general attitude should be:

▶ You have done this many times before and you can comment immediately.

▶ You know precisely what you are all about, so you can have an opinion on the spot.

▶ You know your pricing structures intimately and you can quote the job now.

▶ You are completely on top of your availability and you can talk about timings now.

▶ Overall, you completely understand what they are talking about, and your approach tallies well with their needs.

These are the sorts of qualities that you should be conveying in all your meetings. They will ensure that, more often than not, your meetings are indeed fun. They are also the qualities of a successful person who knows their subject well and has a confident demeanour.

And that person is you.

## Focus points

✳ Secure a meeting, and get organized straightaway.
✳ Get chronological.
✳ Research everything thoroughly.
✳ Give them a list of ways in which you can help.
✳ Include things that you could do, even if you have never done them.
✳ Ask what is on their mind at the moment and offer to fix it.
✳ Listen more than you talk.
✳ Be more positive than everyone else in every meeting.
✳ Never be late.
✳ Be spontaneous and act naturally.

# 9

# Staying sane and relentlessly enthusiastic

**In this chapter you will learn:**

- ► *How to take the issues seriously, but not yourself*
- ► *Why you should not do the same thing for too long*
- ► *The importance of time off and how to build it into your year plan*
- ► *Why hobbies are a great idea*
- ► *How to get your working environment right*

Stay sane and relentlessly enthusiastic? Has the author lost the plot? Surely it can't be possible? Oh yes it can, and here's how.

## Take the issues seriously, but not yourself

This is a maxim that really, really works. Customers want their issues taken seriously, but this doesn't mean that you have to do things in a boring way. Earnest subject matter does not mean that the people dealing with it have to be in a permanent state of melancholy. So relax and don't take it all so seriously.

Humour and lightness of touch are great ways of staying calm and sane. A good laugh can really take the pressure off. On the other hand, being downhearted too frequently makes you annoyed with yourself, and you can be sure that it's no barrel of laughs for those around you either. This is not to suggest that you wear a revolving bow tie and clown suit to your next meeting. But try some of these ideas for lightening up your day:

▶ Take some interesting photos of a hobby or holiday to your next meeting.

▶ Take a customer a small present such as a box of chocolates.

▶ Send them an amusing article or quote from the paper.

▶ Record a programme that you think they might like that has absolutely nothing to do with work.

You get the idea. These are pleasant and interesting things to do. They are not strictly work, but they will make work more enjoyable for you and your customers.

**Remember this: Serious issues, light-hearted you**

Take the issues seriously, but not yourself. You're not that important, honestly. It is quite possible to be grinding through the nastiest business problems and still retain a sense of humour. Customers will hugely appreciate it if you do.

# Never do one thing for too long

It is a rare person who enjoys doing the same thing over and over again for a very long time. That could mean several hours on the same day. It could mean most days of the week for three months, or most weeks of the year for five years. The ratio doesn't matter, but the principle does. Eventually we all get bored. Consequently, it is very important that you never do one thing for too long.

In the context of one working day, it is probably unhelpful for you to do one particular thing for more than a couple of hours. To stay fresh, you should move on to something else unless it is one of those exceptional items that simply has to be churned through from time to time and really does take a long while. Even then, you may still need regular breaks from it, and breaking up any monotonous task is a healthy thing to do.

In any particular working week, you really should not be doing literally the same thing every day. You can keep it up for a while, but not for months. Keep reminding yourself that you are the person in charge. Many who work on their own have deliberately left the strictures of company life precisely to gain greater freedom for themselves. It therefore represents a significant irony if they find that they are constrained in some way by their new circumstances. You may think that you have to do a certain thing, but there is always a chance that you do not. Simply pause to consider it, and if the job is really too horrible, decide whether to find a different way round it or, in extreme cases, whether to turn the task down.

In any working year, if your work is too repetitive, you have almost certainly got the mix wrong. You need to take time out to review what types of work make up your livelihood. Get a large piece of paper and jot down all the types of work you do. Now put a percentage of time spent by each of them. What does this tell you? For example, if you have only two categories on your sheet of paper, then this means that you spend *half a year* doing each. That sounds fairly dull, and if this is indeed the case, then you need to be utterly convinced that you love your subject matter and can keep your enthusiasm levels up every time you are engaged to do such jobs. Even if you have six things on the list, you will still have spent two months on each that year. Are you happy with that? If not, you need to re-engineer how you make your money by making some positive changes. Consider declining work that you have too much of, and finding new ways to stimulate more interesting things to do so that you can have a better mix.

If, when reviewing three years or more of the nature of your work, you conclude that you have been doing the same thing for too long, you have a serious problem. There's no point in embarking on the euphoria and pride of working on your own only to find that you have invented a new but equally boring mousetrap. It really is quite heartbreaking if someone who works on their own says that they are bored and have been for years. It doesn't make any sense at all. Their destiny is in their own hands, so unfortunately one can only conclude that someone who claims this is probably quite boring themselves and does not have the necessary enterprise to change what they do. You need to nip monotony in the bud.

All in all, regardless of what time period you are looking at, this mantra will serve you well:

*'If your work is becoming repetitive, change it.'*

# Don't forget to build time off into your year plan

Staying sane and relentlessly enthusiastic. Mmm. Is this a realistic goal or some sort of nirvana that nobody who works on their own could realistically be expected to achieve?

We'll have a look at the sanity part first. The definition of sanity is 'the state of having a normal healthy mind' or 'good sense and soundness of judgement'.

*'The definition of insanity is doing the same thing over and over again and expecting different results.'*

Benjamin Franklin

We are talking here about the condition of a rational person who feels well balanced and reasonably calm. Many aspects of modern life would appear to be designed to unhinge us at every opportunity, and the pressures of any breadwinner in today's society are well documented. This is precisely why so many people choose to earn their living from a company rather than to generate the income themselves. They welcome the comfort and the safety net that company structures appear to offer. The buildings are provided and so is the pattern of work. Sometimes they receive all sorts of other luxuries – cars, travel allowances, health care, life insurance, and so on. And although it often appears that these parts of the package are there purely for their monetary value, in truth many people value them for their supporting properties as much as their financial value.

In some circles, this debate has moved on so far that you can now find books that ask what companies are for anyway. Some conclude that, whereas many would assume that they are there to make money for the owners, they actually perform a focal role in society and are there to bind people together in a structured way. We have all met people who claim that they couldn't get anything done if it weren't for their partner who organizes everything, whether that's arranging their social life, remembering birthdays or booking a holiday. In a work context, there would appear to be many who could not even do their work without the support services provided by their colleagues – the majority of these colleagues seemingly more junior than them. You know the sort of thing: 'If her secretary wasn't there she wouldn't turn up anywhere.'

You need to engineer a set-up that keeps you sane. How then, do you also remain relentlessly enthusiastic? First of all, enthusiasm is an absolutely fundamental prerequisite of someone who runs their own business. Nobody else is going to generate business for you. No one else is going to be enthusiastic on your behalf. The job falls to you. People don't want to do business with someone who lacks enthusiasm, so one way or another you need to find a way of having an endless supply of the stuff.

▶ Keep lots of variety in what you do to stay fresh.

▶ Get keyed up for phone calls and meetings, and try to be in a good mood before you do them.

- ▶ Change things if you don't find them interesting.

- ▶ Take a sensible amount of time off so that you can return to your work energetically.

The net effect for your customers should be that your enthusiasm *appears* to be relentless even though of course it is impossible for any person to be in that state as a permanent condition. You will have noticed that a vital part of this is taking the right amount of time off work. How many times have you heard a self-employed person say that they haven't had a holiday for ages? Even if they have arranged it and left the country, they still keep worrying about the business when they are lying on a beach somewhere. This is a poor formula that usually leads to some form of meltdown, with both the business and the individual inevitably suffering.

One particularly helpful trick is to build time off into your plan for the year. Don't do it on the fly halfway through. If you do it ad hoc like this, there is a very strong chance that the break that you do go for won't really do the trick. You will almost certainly have compromised on one aspect or another, and this does not befit the reward that you have earned entirely off your own bat. So look at the year and ask yourself these sorts of questions:

- ▶ When are the best times of year to be away?

- ▶ Will you take one large chunk or several smaller bits?

- ▶ Do you need a sabbatical?

- ▶ If so, how would you arrange it?

- ▶ What if you plan a 10-month year instead of 12?

- ▶ Can you arrange the financial aspects now?

- ▶ Where do you want to go?

- ▶ In what sort of style?

- ▶ With anyone else or on your own?

- ▶ What sort of research do you need to do before you can answer some of these questions?

You need to ask a lot of questions. In particular, it pays to consider the financial year that isn't – the way in which companies organize and reorganize time to suit their changing circumstances. For more on this, read another of my books, *So What?* This way, you can plan excellent time off, pre-market the timing of it to your customers, and you do not need to worry about the possible implications when you are away because you have planned the whole thing properly. In addition, the fact that you have put so much thought into your recreational time says volumes about the level of thought that you apply to your customers' business issues. Even better, when you are actually taking the time off, you can relax completely safe in the knowledge that this is *exactly* what you have been working for.

**Remember this: Take time off**

Don't forget to build time off into your year plan. You work to live, right? So don't design a business that has you working all hours and every day of the year. Create something with a little space. Either build it in for small amounts regularly, or large chunks infrequently – whatever suits your style and your business.

# When you take time off, be genuinely unavailable

What is the point of taking a break if you spend a vast amount of it checking messages on your mobile phone or logging on to your email system? It is quite simple to put the measures in place to explain why you are not around before you make yourself unavailable. Also don't forget that corporate time moves differently to normal time, so many of your clients won't even notice that you have gone away anyway (see Chapter 6).

Here is the self-employed person's guide to taking time off and being *genuinely* unavailable:

▶ Put your mobile phone in a drawer and under no circumstances take it with you.

- ▶ Do not check email unless you have a burning need to contact a loved one (try postcards or a landline instead – they worked fine for years).

- ▶ Do not take any work material with you at all.

- ▶ Change the messages on your phones to explain what is going on.

- ▶ Set up an auto response on your email to do the same.

- ▶ Tell your customers a long way in advance that you will not be available (this often means that you actually receive significantly more work before you go so that their needs are covered whilst you are away).

All in all, this approach works really well. There will of course be some lines of work where you really do need to be contactable, but you can judge the level of that for yourself. Suffice to say that if you apply a fraction of the above, you will stand a better chance of having a decent break, and that will be in everybody's interests.

If you doubt that you can do any of this, then you might want to grab a copy of one of my other books, *Tick Achieve,* which explains how.

## Develop new hobbies to alleviate monotony and make yourself more interesting

A topic related to taking time off is the development of hobbies. This is not so that you can spend weeks on end doing the hobby and not working, although there may be some cases whereby what starts life as a hobby purely for pleasure actually becomes income generating. But let's assume for the moment that it is solely for pleasure. What purpose do hobbies serve?

First of all, they have the capacity to alleviate monotony. Take a little break from time to time to do the thing that you want. It could be playing a musical instrument, reading, poetry, painting, sport – anything you like. They can all play an important role in adding variety to your day.

Second, they tend to make people more interesting by adding another dimension to what could otherwise be regarded as simply a 'businessperson'. The more obscure the hobby, the more interesting you become. This makes you more intriguing to talk to, and the fact that you do something constructive in your spare time says volumes about your level of application and your potential to deliver in a business context.

## If you have had a good day, reward yourself

Do bear in mind that when you work on your own, the only person who can reward you is *you*. Naturally, the money you receive for your work is in itself a form of reward, but here we are referring to the more emotional side of things. Occasionally someone will thank you or say well done for something, and that is very nice in its own right. Yet sometimes you need to extend the courtesy to yourself. It's a good discipline because it forces you to review what has been achieved and then decide what level of reward is appropriate in return. Companies do it for their staff – now you need to learn how to do it for yourself.

For example, if you had set yourself a target of doing or achieving x, y and z in a day, and you find that you have done them all successfully (with the outcome you wanted) by lunchtime, consider taking the rest of the day off. Visit a museum, rearrange your wardrobe, go shopping, take a walk, whatever you fancy. Once you have got the hang of the idea, you can apply it to any time period you want:

▶ If you have had a good week, reward yourself.

▶ If you have had a good month, reward yourself.

▶ If you have had a good year, reward yourself.

If you are the sort of person who likes targets as a motivational tool, you might want to fill in these headings and pin them to the wall:

**My rewards**

If I achieve _____today,
I will reward myself with _____

If I achieve _____ this week,
I will reward myself with _____

If I achieve _____ this month,
I will reward myself with _____
_____

If I achieve _____ this year,
I will reward myself with _____

 **Try it now:** Good day = reward

If you have had a good day, reward yourself. You deserve it. Far too many people soldier on for years on end without pausing to remind themselves of what they have achieved. It shouldn't be a permanent slog. Pat yourself on the back occasionally.

# Only over-deliver to a level that reflects your premium price

This is an issue that afflicts many people who run their own businesses. They are so desperate to please that they over-deliver hugely on every job. In the early days, this is reasonably understandable because every business needs a base from which to establish itself, and a job well done frequently leads to another. However, it is not a sustainable state of affairs in the long run. Why not? Because:

▶ Over-delivery equates to underpayment. Whichever way you look at it, you are being paid too little for doing too much.

▶ Work expands to fit the available time. If you haven't got enough to do then spend the spare time on getting more paid work, not doing more on the things for which you are already being paid (too little).

▶ After a while, your customers will become used to the level of service that the over-delivery represents. This is where it all starts to go wrong, and there are only two possible outcomes:

1 They will not want you to put your prices up to reflect the time that you really are spending on their work.
2 The next time you do a job for them, they will expect the same level of over-delivery and will be upset if you do not deliver it.

Either way you are in an awkward position, so don't let it get to that stage. The moral is that you should only over-deliver to the point that reflects your pricing, preferably your premium pricing. This basically means that you should set a relatively high but fair price at the beginning of a job and it then becomes your decision whether to eat into some of your own margin to increase the amount of service you eventually provide. In the end everybody wins with this approach because you have commanded a good price and your customer has had excellent delivery.

**Unlock the facts:** Beware over-delivery

Only over-deliver to a level that reflects your premium price. If you are being well paid for your efforts, then fair enough. But make sure that your customers are not taking advantage of you unreasonably. If you let them do it this time, they will assume it is normal and expect the same thing next time.

# Get your working environment right

One final point with regard to staying sane and enthusiastic: you can't do it if you don't like your working environment. Given that running your own business is a daily process of motivation and reinvention, you cannot hope to achieve this if you don't like where you work. If you work at home, there are all sorts of things that you can do to get comfortable:

▶ Some people like to have a clearly differentiated room to work in where they can spread out, have all their stuff, and generally make a mess. Others only need a desk in the corner of the bedroom. Work out your preferred style.

▶ Decide on the level of tidiness you require about the place and arrange things accordingly.

▶ If you have a partner or other family members around you at home, talk to them about the bits that matter to you. What is out of bounds? Which things do you use in a working context that are in the house? Are there any aspects of other people's clutter and behaviour that prevent you from getting things done? If so, have you found a polite way of discussing it? Once you have mentioned it, they can understand better that the home is also a working environment, and perhaps make a few adjustments to help.

Some people simply cannot work at home. Even though they can work effectively on their own, they require the discipline of a separate place of work to get them in the mood. These types should consider:

▶ Does the place that I work in really reflect my style?

▶ Is my journey to work sensible or is it just as bad as travelling to a company?

▶ Do I get to fraternize with like-minded people, or would I be better off somewhere else?

One way or another, you need to be inspired to get your work done: if your environment isn't right, change it.

So there we have it. Take the work seriously, but not yourself. Don't do the same thing for too long, and take sensible time off, preferably to do something really stimulating. Throw some hobbies into the mix, rather than over-deliver when you aren't being paid enough to justify it. This all adds up to a decent balance that will make you better at everything you do.

Which, of course, will certainly increase your chances of staying sane and appearing, or even truly being, relentlessly enthusiastic.

## Try it now: Your working environment

You need to get this right. You can't lighten up the world from a darkened room. Decide what kind of space and mood you need and set about arranging it. If you work at home, let your family know what the rules are so that you don't end up frustrated.

## Focus points

✳ Take the issues seriously, but not yourself.
✳ Never do one thing for too long.
✳ Don't forget to build time off into your year plan.
✳ Take time off.
✳ When you do, be genuinely unavailable.
✳ Develop new hobbies to alleviate monotony.
✳ Make yourself more interesting.
✳ If you have a good day, reward yourself.
✳ Only over-deliver to a level that reflects your premium price.
✳ Get your working environment right.

# 10

# You are not alone

In this chapter you will learn:

▶ *How to establish your own self-employed network*
▶ *How to say no politely*
▶ *How to refer your surplus work to others*
▶ *How to enjoy the camaraderie of other companies*
▶ *How to blur the lines between work and social life*

Here's an old joke you might enjoy. Three monks are sitting in the desert having taken a lifelong vow of silence. As they sit there in total tranquillity, a small cloud of dust gathers far off on the horizon. After staring at it for seven years, the first monk turns to the one in the middle and says: '*What's that?*'

Seven years later, after no little analysis, the second monk replies: '*I think it's a horse.*'

Seven years after that, the third monk rounds on the other two, exclaiming: '*It's too bloody noisy here. I'm off!*'

Which just goes to show that peace and quiet is a very relative state of affairs. Or, to put it another way, two people are placed on top of two different mountains. One thinks it's a disaster because they can't talk to anyone, the other thinks 'Peace at last'. You get the idea.

## Just because you work on your own, it doesn't mean you are alone

Feeling alone is a state of mind. One person might be happy seeing one other person a day. Another might find that intolerable, and require the company of 20. It rather depends on what you have to do with your time and how needy you are when it comes to interacting with other people. The trick is to keep your head steady and gradually to engineer the pattern of your day, week or month into something that you actively enjoy.

Remember that lots of people are full of admiration for the fact that you work on your own in the first place. They may well envy your ability to go to the shops when you like, declare your own day off from time to time, and not be ordered around by a boss that you may or may not respect. So when you feel a bit isolated, just remind yourself that it is your decision what you do next. It is your choice to decide how often you wish to be 'alone', what to do with any spare time, and how to use it to relax on your own terms, or to contact someone you want.

If someone has lots of friends but happens not to be in anyone's company at a particular moment, to what extent are they 'alone'? For every sole trader who wants to meet more people, there are hundreds of employees in companies yearning for everyone else to go away so that they can get on with their own thing. So the knack is to work out, understand and appreciate all the contacts you have, and all the opportunities there are for interaction with those people, and organize the shape of it to suit your particular preference. These days, this set of interrelationships would probably be called a network.

# Establish your own self-employed network

What is a network anyway? It isn't tangible, so if it does exist, it exists in your mind as a set of contacts organized along whatever lines suit you. Or it may not be organized at all, although when you work on your own that may be a bit too random for your own good. So if you can have a network when you work for a company, and in your social life, then you can certainly have one when you work for yourself.

One crucial thing links everyone who works on their own: they work on their own.

Which means that they all go through what you go through. There are few more unifying features than this one crucial bit of common ground. So whenever self-employed people meet, they usually end up with lots to discuss. The sort of stuff they talk about is often very wide-ranging, precisely because they are juggling all the work and personal issues that this book raises. This may sound self-evident, but consider the number of business meetings between those who work for companies that never get near to touching on their feelings or social lives – the things that *really* matter to them. There are millions of these so-called conversations every day, and they are usually much more one-dimensional than the subject matter when two sole traders meet.

So the conversations between sole traders are wider ranging and have a tremendous capacity to generate genuine empathy. Put simply: you are very likely to sympathize with each other and to get on. That's a good basis for a relationship. You will both want to pay significant attention to what the other is good at, and what they enjoy doing.

This makes sense for three reasons:

▶ You are in the same boat.

▶ You both earn a living by listening to others.

▶ They might be able to help you (the other person will be thinking the same thing).

That's a good equation in anyone's book. If this state of affairs is repeated over multiple conversations for a year or two, you are going to develop a pretty extensive set of contacts with other sole traders with whom you can swap experiences and other contacts.

This applies whether they work in your area or not. Those who do similar work to you will be interesting to meet because you can compare specifics about your field, and they may be very useful to know about when it comes to referring surplus work (see later in this chapter). Self-employed people who do not work in your sector are equally fascinating to talk to. As well as all the general issues that confront those who work on their own, you may well find that it is their very lack of knowledge about your area that makes their comments all the more valuable. You have all heard people say 'I'm too close to it', so this type of encounter offers the equivalent of an objective commentator whose opinions are not biased by what they think they already know about your subject.

Unlike the sales messages we have examined in most parts of the book, this is exactly where social media, email, and online chat rooms come into play. If you use them for this moral support purpose, you are using them well. So now you have a self-employed network.

### Unlock the facts: Your own network

Many people worry about the potential loneliness of the sole trader, but it doesn't have to be. Developing contacts with other self-employed people who experience exactly the same issues as you helps you to stay calm when tricky situations arise. There is a strong chance that the same thing has happened to them. So develop a support network and chat to them regularly.

# Balance the service equation

▶ **Over-service or service over?**

We have already discussed one of the most difficult juggling acts that the sole trader has to carry off. At one end of the spectrum you need to know how to fill in time when you don't have enough work, and at the other you have to work out how to behave when you can't fit it all in. Either extreme is dangerous if not handled sensitively. In Chapter 9 we looked at the economic implications of this. But here we are concerned with those aspects that affect your state of mind.

Take a look at the diagram.

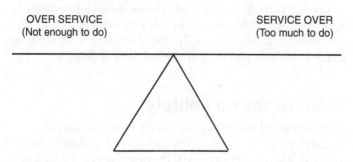

OVER SERVICE
(Not enough to do)

SERVICE OVER
(Too much to do)

**Figure 10.1** Balancing the service equation

Let's look at the over-servicing end first. If you are over-servicing a customer, it may well be because you have spotted a future opportunity and wish to demonstrate a point, or just that you like the work, or the customer. However, there is also a chance that you are doing it because you are filling in the time to ensure that you have plenty of interaction with others. Or, put more bluntly, to stop yourself from being lonely. This isn't a great thing to do. What is happening here is that you are usurping your business requirements with your personal emotional needs. A well-balanced interlocking of the two is a good thing: using your business as an emotional crutch is not.

So pause to consider whether you are using your business too much to support your emotional needs.

If you are, then change the balance, because you can be sure that fairly soon your customers will begin to notice too. That means that they will realize that you are actually not that busy (which will make them question why you are not much in demand), or they will get used to your being constantly available for their every demand (which you will regret later when you do have a lot to do). Either way, you will be creating a situation that is not in your favour.

Now let's look at the 'service over' end. What does it mean? It means that the service you provide is over because you cannot provide what the customer is asking for at the time they want it. Some sole traders go into a flat spin when this happens. Some over promise. Some fudge it. Good ones turn it to their advantage. Does the fact that you cannot do the job precisely when they need it this time mean that they will never be a customer again? Not necessarily. The knack is to work out how to say no politely, and there are lots of ways of doing it.

## Learn to say no politely

People often feel that if they say no, then that's the end of it, and that the person asking the question will end up being annoyed. This doesn't have to be the case. Let's have a look at some of the circumstances in which you might not be able to agree to a customer request:

▶ You haven't got the time.

▶ The price isn't right.

▶ The type of work isn't quite what you like.

▶ You have done so much of the same work recently that you would rather do something else.

▶ You did not enjoy working with them before and would rather not again.

The precise reasons don't really matter. The point is that you need to explain your position in a way that leaves the door open for further business in due course should things change. Why is that? Because at some point in the future:

- ▶ You may well have the time.

- ▶ The price might well be right.

- ▶ The nature of the request from that person may be different.

- ▶ You may not have done that type of work for a while.

- ▶ Your opinion of the customer may have changed.

Everything is constantly changing, and it changes faster when you work on your own than it does in a company. So stay open-minded and let them down politely and gently.

Here are some civilized ways of declining work and some possible reactions.

> *'I'm really sorry, I am fully booked at the moment. Can the deadline be moved back at all?'*

A lot of customers respect the fact that you are busy. It proves that you are successful and in demand, and it reflects and confirms the value of your premium pricing. Anyway, time might not be their main consideration. There will be those who become unhappy, but they often come back at a later date, particularly if they have a less than satisfactory experience elsewhere (which they often do, particularly if they go for a 'quick fix' alternative).

> *'I'm really sorry, I have just completed a massive programme of exactly that sort of work, and I have decided to take a breather from it before taking on any more.'*

Customers always want people to be fresh and keen on their subject matter, so your reaction is honest and reasonable. It might not suit their immediate needs, but it is representative of a respectful attitude. They might not like it, but then again they may come back to you later with requests for different types of work that you would enjoy more.

> *'I'm really sorry, I am fully booked at the moment. May I refer you to someone else who does the same sort of work, who may be able to do it for you? I know them well and think they would offer a suitable alternative.'*

This is a very constructive response, and they will probably thank you for it because it is a very professional thing to do. It proves that you are 'big' enough to pass work on. It also shows that you have a good working knowledge of your market to go with your magnanimous attitude. The contact you refer them to will certainly thank you too (see next section). If you are incredibly unlucky, they will commission your contact to do the work, prefer them to you, and give them all their future work. So you will have lost a customer. But that's pretty unlikely. Now read on.

**Try it now:** Say no politely

Many people hate saying no, but if you fail to develop the knack, you could ruin your business. You might end up with too much work, inappropriate work, and all sorts of other chaos. You're the boss, so you decide what's right for the business. It is not rude. It allows you to manage your business properly, so learn to say no politely.

# Refer your surplus work to others

How would you feel if the phone rang and there was someone on the line offering you work? Not a full-time job, you understand, just a really decent project of the type where you usually have to invest a lot of time to secure it. This time, the pre-sale work has all been done, and they are offering it to you. There could be lots of reasons. They are too busy to do it themselves. They are going on holiday. They were asked about it, but it isn't precisely what they are best at. So they call to ask if you would be interested.

It's a great feeling, and it happens when you have let other sole traders know what you do, and when you have offered to help them if they ever get stuck. It works both ways. You may well have been in the same position yourself and referred some work to them some time in the past. Whatever the reason, it is one of the most cost-effective calls you will ever receive, apart from a dream customer ringing out of the blue precisely when you want, proposing exactly what you like, at the right price.

So this is a 'golden phone call', and they really can work in both directions. You are not alone as a sole trader precisely because these calls move back and forth between well-connected self-employed people all the time. They come about because you have presented your skills well, been thoughtful in introducing contacts to each other, and probably because you have already generated business for the person who is calling you now. Even better, these calls are completely free. They involve none of the usual investment of time and effort that most new business pursuits do. And once you have set the ball rolling, they start working their way back to you.

Sometimes these interrelationships can progress a step further by turning into proper working alliances and subcontracting arrangements. This can be good or bad, depending on how you handle things. Having an overflow facility for your business is good, and so is picking up work from contacts when you have not had to over-invest in securing it. On the downside, these arrangements can take a lot of time and maintenance, so you have to keep a very close eye on whether they are taking up too much of your time in relation to the work they actually generate. The self-employed world is littered with examples of people who talk a good game about networks and alliances, but when you dig deeper you often find that they spend too much time feeding the arrangement to justify the negligible amount of work that it creates. By all means develop your contacts, but don't fall into this trap.

# Enjoy the camaraderie of other companies

Here's another very good reason why you are not alone. We have already looked at how you can generate a culture even when you work on your own. So it stands to reason that a company with two or more people in it will also have its own culture. This usually happens the moment those two people decide to take a break and go to the pub. By the time there is a full payroll, all sorts of social activities start to develop. Banter in reception. Jokes around the coffee machine. A quick drink after work. Sporting challenges. Mutual hobbies. The bigger the company, the more there is of it. And chances are that many of your customers are just such companies. Which means that there is a hybrid of business and social life waiting out there for you to join when you need it.

In other words, not all of your entertainment has to be generated by you. Although as a sole trader you will become a master of creating almost everything yourself, this does not necessarily have to apply to the human company that you may need in order to stay sane (we came up with enough of these in the last chapter). There are actually hundreds of enjoyable opportunities lurking within many of your customer relationships, so it is your job to work out what type and frequency of interaction provides you with the right balance. Chances are that these social interactions will have a positive bonding effect on your customer relationships too.

Just a couple of words of warning though: under no circumstances allow yourself to become known as a party freeloader. This advice is not an excuse to gatecrash scores of customer parties and gain a reputation for coasting on their hospitality. Use your judgement to join in with those activities that you enjoy, and which are appropriate in the context of your business relationship with the customer.

## Blur the lines between work and social life

Is it likely that self-employed people generate a lot of business out of social situations? Certainly. In fact, one of the main points about working for yourself is that there should be less of a distinction between work and social life. The old-fashioned lines of demarcation between work and play should become more vague as your solo life becomes more established. You know the sort of thing that represents a regimented life: alarm goes, leave home, use public transport, enter place of work, begin work. Do the whole thing in reverse at the end of the day. Begin social life.

This is precisely what you left a company to avoid, or why you never joined one in the first place. So it doesn't make much sense to set up a whole new set of equally pointless boundaries in your new life. We have discussed some of these parameters already. 'Introduce some humanity into your CV' in Chapter 4 was all about laying the ground for a respectful interplay between your private and business life. 'Develop new hobbies to alleviate monotony and make yourself more interesting' in Chapter 9 was all about broadening your appeal by diversifying your interests so that they imply how sharp you are as a businessperson. Here, we are going one step further and blurring the lines between work and social life.

We already know that you can't permanently be in work mode, but equally of course you can't be in constant play mode either. However, what you can do is take a more relaxed view about whether you are 'on duty' or not. This does not cut only in favour of relaxing more. It also means that when you are socializing, you may equally be 'working'. The balance you create here is really important. It doesn't have to be arduous either way. That's why you need to have your antenna scanning for work opportunities, common areas, contacts, ideas, and so on, but all in a relaxed social context. Don't force it or get uptight. Keep it loose and stay open-minded.

You really never do know when an amazing opportunity is lurking in the next enjoyable night out.

**Remember this:** Blur work and social life

Imagine a world in which you could do all your business whilst spending time in the company of people you like. It is possible. Let your friends know what you do for work, and let your customers know what you do in your spare time. Then mix up the two. When you do, work doesn't feel like work any more.

## View it like an extended family

How often do you see the members of your family? The answer to this question varies enormously by individual. Some people live next door to their family members and see them all the time. Some have emigrated and are lucky to see them once a year. Somewhere in the middle lies a mixture of contact points and frequencies that the family members work out amongst themselves. You will know roughly how often you speak to your parents, siblings, grandparents, cousins, and so on, and in return, so will they.

Your business contacts can be viewed in exactly the same way so that you can judge the appropriate frequency that suits the relationship. Once you have thought about this, you will have unwittingly designed a latticework of contact points that prove conclusively that you are not alone. If you remain uncertain, do the old trick of writing it down. The proof will be there in front of you.

The family analogy may also help you to classify some of your contacts. Who are the 'must call once a week' customers? Who are the less well-known relations who are happy to chat once every few months? Once you get the hang of it, you can extend the metaphor from phone calls to meetings, anniversaries, parties – pretty much any interaction that has a bearing on the business but that can spill into a social setting.

## If you stay in touch, they will too

As with all pieces of general advice, this assertion is only half true. Although there are always some people in the world who never seem to return calls, cards or invitations, most people do. If you really do have some hopeless contacts that never get in touch, then you should seriously consider whether they are worth staying in touch with at all. Think about it. If they don't call back, then you are clearly not doing business together. If that is consistently the case, then why bother with these people? We examined in Chapter 5, 'Taming the telephone', what to do if potential customers refuse to take your calls and concluded that, even if they eventually did, they would probably be a nightmare to deal with anyway. So you can cut out a lot of soul-destroying heartache if you weed out such contacts.

But let's be more optimistic and assume that most right-minded people do stay in touch. Once you get rolling with your 'keep in touch' programme, it will start to generate contacts in return without you actually doing anything. You will soon discover that you are not the sole initiator of an outbound contact programme. Don't forget that other people will be doing exactly the same thing. And don't forget the first point in this book: *Assume that you have something to offer.*

The number of people with whom you stay in touch, and the frequency with which you do so, is critical. We looked at the business implications of this balance in Chapter 2, 'The right tools for the job', and we introduced the idea of the Pester Line to prevent you from irritating potential customers unduly. But here we are interested in the other side of the equation. You must not fritter away your energy by frequently contacting people who won't keep in touch with you in return. It's a total waste of your time, and that ultimately means money. So it is important that you review regularly the people with whom you stay in touch, and whether it is worth your while. At the beginning, you need to develop an initial pool of contacts, and of course until you have attempted to stay in touch with someone for a reasonable period, you won't know what their track record is in this department. But as soon as you realize that they never really bother to stay in touch and so do not represent any kind of business opportunity, then you need to seriously consider whether they should be dropped from your contact list.

## One man's solitary confinement is another man's freedom

So do you really still think that you are alone? One would hope by now that you don't really believe it, but let's finally nail the point anyway. Solitary confinement is one way of viewing self-employment, and splendid isolation is another. It all depends on your perspective. It doesn't take a genius to work out that the successful sole trader will choose to see it as the latter. Now that you work on your own, your job is to be an optimistic self-starter. You are free to do what you like, when you like. You are not in the slightest bit alone. In fact, there is a strong chance that you lead a far less isolated life than many of those who mingle with hundreds of people every day. That's because you are doing it on your terms.

Never forget why you first went self-employed or why you are seriously considering it now. You want to do things your way. That means you are in charge. You decide how much thinking time you need. How much peace and quiet. How much action.

And how much interaction. You can meet as many people as you like, or as few. You can have hugely socially interactive days, and really quiet, peaceful ones. You can mix them up to your liking. It's great! There are people in corporations all over the world who would be highly envious of that level of freedom. So make it work for you, and enjoy it.

## Unlock the facts: Solitary confinement or freedom?

One man's solitary confinement is another man's freedom. Hermits should get out more. Relentless socialites should pause and think occasionally. Choose a balance that suits you between solitary and sociable work, so that you are neither a workaholic nor a loner.

## Focus points

✳ Accept that, although you work on your own, you are not alone.
✳ Establish your own self-employed network.
✳ Balance the service equation.
✳ Learn to say no politely.
✳ Refer your surplus work to others.
✳ Enjoy the camaraderie of other companies.
✳ Blur the lines between work and social life.
✳ View it like an extended family.
✳ Stay in touch, so they will too.
✳ Make your choice: solitary confinement or freedom?

# Part Two

## Developing and Growing Your Business

# 11

# Reviewing your business: some nasty questions

In this chapter you will learn:

▶ *What to do when things go wrong*

▶ *How to struggle with the issue of what now?*

▶ *That you cannot be prescriptive about survival or growth*

▶ *How to apply some tough thinking*

▶ *How to pose some nasty questions such as, so what?*

# What to do when things go wrong

It's a tricky business. What exactly do you do when your business is not going as you wish? Difficult times require difficult decisions, based on solid thinking. Panicking is no use, and nor is fruitless worrying. So don't rush into a blue funk and assume that the world is ending. Stay calm and review your business and your options as coolly as you possibly can, even if you are not happy with the circumstances. Stick to the facts and be as objective as possible. Check with respected friends or partners whether your thinking is veering off into strange areas, and take heed of their wise words to self-correct.

**Remember this:** When things go wrong

Don't panic. Things go wrong in business all the time. Pause to think carefully, stay calm and take advice if necessary. Then decide what to do.

# You cannot be prescriptive about survival or growth

Although this book contains advice, it does not attempt to prescribe exactly how your business can survive or grow by following a fixed pattern. You need to be open-minded, and cherry-pick the ideas that best suit your circumstances. Growth in particular is always an adventure, and it needs to be viewed as such, and approached with the right attitude.

*'An adventure is an inconvenience rightly considered.'*
G. K. Chesterton

Rushing into the unknown is all part of the thrill of running a business. It is all a bit of an adventure. Some people love it. Some crave it. Some find themselves in charge of businesses but didn't necessarily ask to be there. Businesses always have issues and problems. You can't have customers without having to sort out a lot of tricky stuff. You can't have staff without having to maintain them. So let's assume that you are in charge of a business. It doesn't matter whether you set it up yourself, or whether someone else did. The point is, it has been up and running for a while, and the launch phase is complete. The business is established. So what are you going to do now?

**Unlock the facts: Too prescriptive?**

Don't get too formulaic about survival and growth. Life's a mess. Adapt. Change something, and do it fast.

## Time for tough love and some tough thinking

You'll have heard of tough love, when people need to be told the truth for their own good. Well now's the time for some tough thinking. That means more confrontation. Not with other people, but with the conflicting thoughts in your head. This tough thinking may apply to you personally, or to your business, and this book contains ways to approach both areas, because they are always interlinked. It is time to confront your demons. This is the basic dilemma all businesses face when they have set up, and have then paused to reflect or have become restless. Let's start with a series of nasty questions that require candid answers. If you think you are not going to like some of the answers, then take some quiet time out and don't attempt the process when you are at work. And please, don't lie to yourself – it renders the whole exercise pointless and you are a grown-up now! Okay, take a deep breath.

**Try it now: Tough love**

It's time for tough love and some tough thinking. Don't dodge the facts, and don't kid yourself. You need a warts-and-all appraisal of your trading conditions, coupled with appropriate remedies.

Some nasty questions:

▶ Are you happy?

▶ Are you in charge of your own destiny?

▶ Are you king of nothing?

- ▶ Are you proud of what you have achieved?

- ▶ Are you impressed with yourself?

- ▶ Are you status conscious?

- ▶ Are you out of your depth?

- ▶ Where does it all end?

- ▶ When does it all end?

What sort of answers have you come up with? This is not a psychological test, so there are no right and wrong ones, but what is the general shape? If you are essentially happy, and in charge of your own destiny, then you might as well stop reading this and go out for a celebratory meal immediately. If you conclude that you are king of nothing, then there is something wrong. If you find yourself in a top role purely for status reasons, or if you feel out of your depth, then we certainly have some work to do. If you have no idea when or where the whole thing is going to end, don't panic. That might not be the end of the world, but it is preferable if you can answer one or the other of them. If you can picture where it is all going to end, but not when, that's a good start because you know what you want but aren't too concerned about the immediate time frame. If you can envisage when you are going to conclude this thing, but not necessarily where, that could be okay. If you are not sure of either, some thought is required.

## Try it now: Nasty questions

The nastier the better. Put yourself and your business right under the microscope. What's the verdict? If you can't be ruthless enough, get someone else to interrogate you.

In another of my other books I extol the virtues of asking yourself simple questions and being brutally honest about the answers. One of the most powerful of these is: So what? Although potentially annoying if addressed to someone else, it is a great leveller when you ask it of yourself. Try some of these for size (for over 200 more, read my book, *So What?*).

**Some 'so what?' questions:**

▶ You're in charge. So what?

▶ You have lots of people reporting to you. So what?

▶ You have a large office. So what?

▶ You have your name on the door. So what?

▶ You are your own boss. So what?

▶ You earn more money than before. So what?

▶ Your sales are up this year. So what?

▶ Your profit is up on last year. So what?

You get the idea. There is no right or wrong answer, but hopefully you have stirred yourself up a bit. The knack is not to give any particular answer, but to know *why* you have given that answer. If you do know why, and are happy with that response, then excellent. If you are not happy with any particular answer, then you have some thinking to do on that topic. Once you get the hang of it, you can invent your own questions, so long as they are all personal to you, and so long as all the responses that you give are honest. Do not fall into the trap of self-delusion.

### Unlock the facts: So what?

It sounds like a dismissive question but that's the point. All those things you think are vital and take for granted in your business: So what? There may be a case for thinking again.

# Can't get no satisfaction

Most people who run businesses are never quite satisfied, because they always feel they have unfinished business, no matter how well things are going. There's always something else that can be done. They are constantly dealing with an unfinished article. They may also be dealing with post-launch blues, or going through a three-year itch. 'Three-year itch' is of course a catch-all phrase for any kind of period of dissatisfaction, and the timing of it varies hugely, as we will see in Chapter 16. For some it is three months, for some seven years, and for some it never comes at all. But if it does, it can eat away as insidious self-doubt, and it needs to be confronted urgently before it starts to ruin everything – that is the business and your sanity.

*'Self-pity is the enemy of generosity.'*
Alexander Chancellor

So what happens if you discover that, on reflection, you are not that happy with your state of affairs? Well, you have got some work to do. There is no room for self-pity here. Your friends and family won't enjoy it, nor will your staff if you have them and, ultimately, it is of no use to you either. So you need to understand why you are not happy, and set about trying to fix it.

*'Do not weep; do not wax indignant. Understand.'*
Baruch Spinoza

The key to this is *understanding*. There is no point sitting around bewailing the fact that things are as they are, when you could be spending time working out why they are as they are. Therein lies the potential to change things. Get to the heart of the matter, and concentrate on which bits you can influence personally, and who can help you attend to the rest. It is the solution you are after, not the waffle and preamble that takes you longer to get there. So spot the endgame, and head for that point straightaway.

*'Almost every man wastes part of his life in attempts to display qualities that he does not possess.'*
Samuel Johnson

Part of the reason may be that you are trying to do things that you do not enjoy, or that you are not particularly good at. There is no disgrace in not being brilliant at everything. In fact, there is barely anyone alive who is. So don't beat yourself up about it. Instead work out ways to circumnavigate areas that don't suit you, re-engineer the business so that you don't have to do them, or get other people in to do them for you. That might be staff, or one-off experts. Have a look at Chapters 4 to 6 for effective ways to tackle this area.

> *'Even in slight things, the experience of the new is rarely without some stirring of foreboding.'*
>
> Eric Hoffer

A lot of people do not like change. Indeed, they are often scared of it. There is nothing wrong with that feeling. So long as you don't allow it to be so overwhelming that it genuinely prevents you from any sort of forward motion. If you run your own business, you should be keen to move ever onward. If you run someone else's, equally you will not want to be doing the same thing all the time, so plunge in to the new with a sense of adventure. You might surprise yourself.

## Focus points

* Are you being too prescriptive about your survival and growth plans?
* Have you decided what to do next?
* Do you regard the next step as an adventure?
* Have you asked yourself the tricky questions?
* Have you confronted the answers you didn't like?
* Have you thoroughly understood why things are as they are?
* Do you know what you are going to do to make things better?
* Have you eliminated any self-pity?
* Have you found solutions to cover for qualities you do not have?
* Have you braced yourself for some tough thinking?

# 12

# The discipline to develop

In this chapter you will learn:

▶ *How to take a new look at your business*
▶ *If your new company is the same as the old company*
▶ *How to rip up the straitjackets you built yourself*
▶ *That efficiency is a sophisticated form of laziness*
▶ *If you are suffering from attitude sickness*

I once met an accountant in Kent. He was a very thoughtful guy, clearly intelligent, and seemingly successful. He had left a larger accountancy practice to set up his own because he felt there was definitely a better way. Excellent. This is the sort of flair and determination that keeps business vital. I then test-drove on him one of my theories about how people approach the administrative aspects of their new businesses, and asked: 'How did you design the administrative systems in your new venture?' The answer held little surprise. 'Oh,' he said, 'we based them on the ones from my previous place.'

This anecdote is not designed to humiliate the man in question, but simply to illustrate one of the oldest pitfalls in the book. That is to say, many people who strike out for a brave new dawn simply end up generating their own version of what they had before, complete with all its flaws and drawbacks. It isn't always the case, but it often is.

# New company: same as the old company?

For those of you who like a bit of rock music, you will be familiar with the line in the The Who song 'Won't Get Fooled Again': 'Meet the new boss. Same as the old boss.' You would do well to ask yourself whether this has inadvertently become the case with you personally, or the company you now run. On reflection are you simply replicating the past? Have you invented a genuinely new mousetrap, or is it unnervingly similar to the old one? So here they come again – more nasty questions.

> *'The truth will set you free, but first it will piss you off.'*
> Gloria Steinem

▶ Is your company unnervingly similar to the one you left because you were supposedly fed up with it?

▶ Have you started behaving similarly to your old boss?

▶ Did you rather lazily imitate the processes and systems at your previous company when designing your current ones?

▶ Do you have a nagging suspicion that certain things around here do not work particularly well?

▶ Do you suspect that there is a better way of doing these things?

▶ Can you think of what they might be?

If the answer to any of these questions is yes, then we have some work to do. It's all about instilling the discipline, both mental and structural, that will free you up to do the rewarding bits more easily and frequently. That's what the question (Are you disciplined enough to survive?) is all about. It means getting rid of any straitjackets that are preventing you or your business from having a decent time of it and being a reasonable success. These straitjackets might be mental, they might be physical, or they might be process-based. Let's have a look at the different types.

# Ripping up the straitjackets you built yourself

What's all this about then? Surely, I hear you cry, I haven't built any straitjackets for myself? Well you won't have done it intentionally, but you may have done it nevertheless. What we are referring to here is something that severely limits or restricts you personally, or an aspect of your business. When you think about it, there may be more of them than you would initially like to admit.

**Straitjacket** (*noun*): a severe limitation or restriction

Grab a pen and paper, and write these three headings on it, leaving space in the middle to fill out your answers.

1 Mental straitjackets

2 Physical straitjackets

3 Process straitjackets

Have a look at each, and write down your instinctive reaction to what these might be. If none occurs, this could be very good news in that you may well be a highly liberated person, free of constraints, running a business that is brilliantly designed and operates perfectly. How many people do you know in that position? More likely, you have reservations and concerns about all sorts of issues. If the page is blank, or you have already finished with your initial thoughts, then try these prompts.

## MENTAL STRAITJACKETS

▶ Do I have time to generate new ideas?

▶ Am I capable of originating new ideas?

▶ If not, do I know anyone who is that can help?

▶ Am I able to implement all the ideas I want?

## PHYSICAL STRAITJACKETS

▶ Is my working environment appropriate?

▶ Do I have the right blend of staff or colleagues?

▶ Do I spend too much time travelling?

▶ Am I frequently in the wrong place to get things done?

## PROCESS STRAITJACKETS

▶ Do I spend too much time in meetings?

▶ Do our systems work well?

▶ Do things get bogged down unnecessarily too often?

▶ Did I design these systems myself, or were they borrowed from somewhere else?

▶ Do they genuinely represent the right tools for the job?

If the answers to these questions do not fill you with glee, then chances are it is time to rip up some straitjackets. If that fills you with dread, it shouldn't. Change is good. Trust your instincts. If you know in your heart that something doesn't work very well, and you now have the courage to confess it unwittingly on paper by answering the questions honestly, then it is time for action. Reassure yourself with the knowledge that, whatever it is, it is broken, and it does need fixing. Once you have taken a deep breath and fixed it, you will have far less hassle from that moment on. Of course, this part of the process only forces you to identify the trouble, not cure it. If you are an excellent problem solver, then you may immediately know how to design your own new mousetrap.

**Try it now:** Ripping up straitjackets

Lots of people set up their own business only to replicate all the nasty problems that frustrated them in their previous job. If you did this, it's time to reconsider and rip up the straitjackets you built yourself.

> *'Reality is the leading cause of stress among those in touch with it.'*
>
> Lily Tomlin

It takes guts to answer the nasty questions honestly. It takes discipline and determination to do something as a result to improve things. This is your job because you are in charge. Whether that is in charge of 100 people or just yourself doesn't make a jot of difference. It's still down to you. Scary? Perhaps, but it shouldn't be. You are either paid well to do precisely that, or you are doing something because of what you believe in. Either way, it's your job, and the main beneficiary will usually be you. If you take the tough medicine now, you will have a more pleasant time in the future.

We have all heard the maxim 'Work to live or live to work?' Which applies to you? Do you work mindlessly because it's there? Or do you use your work as a means to a more fulfilling life? Assuming you would prefer the latter, you need to apply strong discipline to get the business working for you, not the other way round. Let's try another one: 'Rule to work or work to rule?' Do you let the strictures of working practices constrain your ability to enjoy working life and flourish in it? Or do you master the situation and make it work for you? The choice is yours. If by any chance it is the former, then I am afraid you may have turned native.

## Turning native

What does this mean? It means that you have lost the capability to think independently. It means that you sound and act just like everybody else. The old joke goes like this: when management consultants have been working with their clients for too long, if you look at a video of a meeting between them, with no prior knowledge of who is who, you will not be able to differentiate between the consultants and the clients.

Why? Because they are all speaking the same language. Using the same jargon. Wearing the same clothes. The consultants have turned native and are losing their value to their customers. If this is happening to you and your colleagues, change it immediately.

> *'When two people in business always agree, one of them is unnecessary.'*
>
> William Wrigley Junior

It's true isn't it? Under-confident people fail to express their opinion whilst simultaneously failing to recognize that their opinion is precisely what they are paid for. This is true of everybody – staff and consultants. If you don't have a view, what are you there for? So, make sure that you are disciplined enough not to turn native, and that you stay true to your opinions.

> *'An optimist sees an opportunity in every calamity.*
> *A pessimist sees a calamity in every opportunity.'*
>
> Winston Churchill

So we have spent some time looking at the tethers and straitjackets that constrain your business. You should now be turning your mind to how you can liberate yourself and your business systems to get on and enjoy a better work–life balance. Churchill had a point. What do you see? Glass half empty? Or half full? Or, indeed, do you give a stuff about the supposed glass at all? And what's in the glass, by the way? Methylated spirits or champagne? Life is random, and it is almost impossible to plan. So there will be calamities pretty much every day of the week. But that doesn't mean it's the end of the world, and it doesn't mean you can't generate something positive out of it. So it is your job to engineer an opportunity out of whatever circumstances confront you. That's what this phase is all about: confrontation. That means confronting yourself, and the realities of your business.

## Unlock the facts: Turning native

Have you turned yourself or your company into the very thing you used to hate? Creeping bureaucracy? Slow, flabby processes? Lack of energy and enthusiasm? If so, you may have turned native.

# Growing panes: a new look through the business window

Here's a little exercise that might help disentangle the good and bad bits of your working life and your business practices. You've heard of SWOT analysis, and various systems of analysis such as the Boston Matrix. Well this is the world's simplest one. Take a piece of paper and draw a windowpane on it. On the vertical axis, write GOOD at the top, and BAD at the bottom. On the horizontal axis, write OLD on the left, and NEW on the right. Now take a little time to categorize your habits and techniques. If something you usually do is old and good, then it goes in the top left quadrant, and so on. You will quickly build up a picture of the proportion of good/bad/old/new approaches that you use. Now do the same for those of your business.

If you have several practices in the 'Good and Old' segment, then that is fine. They have obviously stood the test of time, and do the job.

If you have several of them in the 'Good and New' section, even better. This means you are generating new ideas that really work. A blend of old and new is healthy, because it suggests good thinking at the outset, followed by fresh ideas thereafter.

If there is anything in the 'New and Bad' area, it needs careful analysis. It takes guts to reject an idea or process that has only recently been introduced. But surgery here may well be necessary. There may be a case for concluding that the jury is still out so a decision should be given a little more time. But more likely than not, the bad item will remain bad no matter how long you leave it, and the sooner it goes the better. This type of decision can be unpopular, particularly if colleagues have a vested interest, but a bad, ineffective process or idea is just that, and it needs to be eliminated quickly.

Anything in the 'Old and Bad' quadrant is clearly a disaster and has to go immediately.

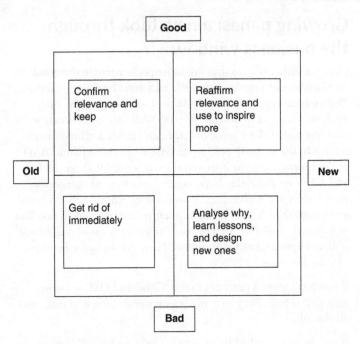

**Figure 12.1** The growing pane.

*'Planning is for the poor.'*

Robert Evans

I have put this quote in to spark a debate. Personally I think it is rubbish. Working out what you want to do and then sorting it out is one of the great fundamentals of having a decent life and a sane mind. You don't have to have endless spreadsheets or spend months over it. Just work out what you want to do, and then do it. The time you dedicate to thinking about things will serve you well when you have to get on and do whatever you have decided. But don't spend too long over it. Trust your instincts. You only have to do three things. It is a fairly straightforward business to write down, but somewhat harder to do. Here they are:

1 Get your head straight.

2 Decide what you want to do.

3 Do it.

**Try it now:** Growing panes

All businesses have growing pains, and often reduction pains. It's time to take a new look through the business window, and see what remedies your business needs.

# Efficiency is a sophisticated form of laziness

Think about it carefully. The more sorted you are, the less you need to panic. We will pursue the idea further in Chapter 17. It is such a simple notion. Get the functional elements organized, and the rest slots into place. However, this level of organization will only be of limited use if your head isn't in the right place. Your attitude has to be right too.

**Remember this:** Efficiency and laziness

Efficiency is a sophisticated form of laziness. Think about it. The better you are at getting things done, the more time you free up to do what you want.

# Are you suffering from attitude sickness?

In order to think clearly, you have to have a decent blend of passion and dispassion. If you are horribly biased, you will make poor decisions. Rose-tinted spectacles are as useless as outright cynicism. You need a balance, otherwise you will become a danger to yourself. Sounds extreme? Not really. Poor thought leads to unsuccessful management and unsuccessful businesses, and you do not want that state of affairs on your hands. It is all about keeping the mystery alive. In the next chapter, we are going to develop some ways of doing this, but meanwhile, take a moment to reflect on the nasty questions in this chapter and Chapter 11, and consider whether you have genuinely confronted the awkward stuff. Confront the tough issues and ask yourself: Am I disciplined enough to survive? Don't fudge the answer. If you do, you won't get anywhere, and you probably won't survive.

*'Anything can happen in life, especially nothing.'*
Michel Houellebecq

## Unlock the facts: Attitude sickness?

Have you become jaundiced about your business? Your staff? Your customers? If so, it is time to take yourself in hand and start afresh. Your business will not survive if your attitude is wrong.

## Focus points

* Are your 'new' approaches the same as your old ones?
* If so, what are you going to do about it?
* Have you identified any mental, physical or process straitjackets?
* If so, what are you going to do about it?
* Have you turned native?
* If so, what are you going to change, and how?
* Have you filled out the Growing Panes grid?
* Have you got rid of any bad things it revealed?
* What have you done about being more organized?
* Is your attitude right?

# 13

# Thinking is free

**In this chapter you will learn:**

- ▶ *That thinking is free, so do it more often*
- ▶ *Why the next big thing might be small*
- ▶ *That a strategy is simply when you have decided what to do*
- ▶ *KISS: Keep It Simple and* Sensible
- ▶ *KITSCH: Keep It Terribly Simple and Cool Headed*
- ▶ *To try again if something doesn't work*

# Thinking is free, so do it more often

*'I haven't had time to think.'*

How many times have we heard that said? Millions of people say it every day in all walks of life, let alone in business. What does it actually mean? If you analyse the phrase carefully, it is complete nonsense. Every sentient being spends the entire day thinking, absorbing circumstances and reacting to them. Of course, the phrase is not literal. What it really means is:

> *'I haven't had time to pause and think about the things that really matter, because lots of irrelevant stuff has got in the way.'*

Aha. That's more accurate, and because businesses usually generate vast amounts of irrelevant stuff, businesspeople are very prone to the problem of not having enough thinking time. This is a tragedy, and it is your job to create the appropriate time to rectify the position. Why is this so important? Because, although you may claim that you are too busy to create the time, if you haven't worked out whether what you are doing is the right thing, then you may only be busy pursuing all the wrong things.

So now is the time to get thinking. It is a free activity. All you have to do is set aside the time and create the appropriate conditions. Some people like total peace and seclusion, others like something to shake them up. Work out your style by answering these questions to help you develop different ways of creating thinking time. Are you likely to have some decent ideas if you:

▶ Sit on top of a mountain

▶ Have a massage

▶ Get on the running machine

▶ Visit an art gallery

▶ Disappear to a country cottage

▶ Drink a bottle of quality wine

▶ Go for a bike ride

▶ Leave the country for the day

- ▶ Take a ride in a hot air balloon

- ▶ Visit the zoo

- ▶ Go fishing?

You get the idea. The activity or circumstance doesn't matter, so long as it is different from where you normally are, and what you normally do.

> *'A great many people think they are thinking, when they are merely rearranging their prejudices.'*
>
> William James

If everything is too samey, or things aren't going that well, it's time for a re-think. And that does not mean rearranging your prejudices, or dreaming up new reasons to prove that you are right about something. It means taking a hard look at what you've got and working out whether it is any good or not, and whether you like your circumstances. If you have any doubts about any aspect of your life or business, it has to be done. Even in the unlikely event that you don't have any concerns at all about anything, it is still a great thing to do. Everything can always be made better or more stimulating.

### Remember this: Thinking is free

Thinking is free, so do it more often. It is amazing the number of people who do things without knowing why. Remove yourself from the hurly burly of day-to-day life, even for an hour, and think.

## Try this: it might just work

You have to enter the thinking process in the right frame of mind. It's no use being petrified, depressed, cynical, paranoid, resentful, jaded or any other negative emotion. It is okay to be a bit vexed or concerned. It is all right to be mildly sceptical. It is fine to be quizzical. In fact, that should positively be encouraged. Your objective should be to let a little light in on your circumstances and view them as though you were someone else looking at you. Strange, and quite detaching, but ultimately rewarding. Start with some general questions:

- How well is the business doing?

- What are the prospects for survival?

- Do you want evolution or revolution?

- Are you facing hard or soft decisions?

- Are you planning the 'next big thing'?

Be positive. You have to believe, 'If I try this, it might just work.'

**Try it now: It might work**

Too many people pre-judge whether something is going to work or not, particularly if they tried it before and it wasn't a success. Don't fall into this trap. Try things out. You never know. If it doesn't work, try something else. Never stop doing this. Otherwise your business will stagnate.

# Why the next big thing might be small

A lot of people get hung up on planning the 'next big thing'. But who is to say that the next big thing has to be big? Sometimes tiny increments of change make amazing things happen. If you are unconvinced of this, read Malcolm Gladwell's book, *The Tipping Point*. It demonstrates how little things can make a big difference, if cunningly applied. If you can't be bothered to buy the book or, rather more importantly, actually read the thing, then you will find a summary of it in the appendix. So don't panic about the fear that you need to come up with something outstandingly original. People rarely do. Occasionally someone like Edison will invent a light bulb, but that's a bit beyond our remit here. If by any chance you are a genius, then put this book down immediately – there's nothing I can teach you.

*'God is in the details.'*

Anonymous artist

There has been a huge amount of hoo-ha about 'the big idea'. Nothing wrong with that, but when you run a business, there is also great mileage to be had from lots of little ideas. Little ideas are great. They are less difficult to come up with, they are usually cheaper and easier to implement, and they can be done more quickly. This enables you to work out rapidly whether they are any good or not. No one wants to admit that a big idea is rubbish once it has been implemented, so they are hard to rectify even if everybody can see that they aren't working very well. An example of this would be when Coca-Cola replaced their original version with a new one. Eventually they had to reissue it as Coke Classic. They got it right in the end, but it took a while for anyone to admit that the new 'big idea' wasn't working. In comparison, little ideas can be test-driven constantly, refined, enlarged, developed or withdrawn with the minimum of fuss. Try making your next big thing small. You might surprise yourself.

**Unlock the facts:** The next big thing

The next 'big thing' might be small. Little developments can make a big difference. They are also a lot less scary to embark on. So try lots of little things.

# A strategy is when you have decided what to do

Complicated thinking is another cul-de-sac. Do not fall into the trap of thinking that an idea needs to be complicated, or that your route to it needs to be either. Good ideas are usually simple, as is the means by which they are conceived. Most people have heard of the KISS acronym, Keep It Simple Stupid. Whilst I admire the sentiment behind it, I am not a fan of the Stupid bit. You are not stupid, nor are most people who run businesses. So I have taken the double liberty of both adapting KISS, and inventing a new one: KITSCH. Here they are.

## KISS: Keep It Simple and Sensible

It's the sensible bit that makes the difference for me. You're not daft, and you instinctively know what is likely to work. So keep it sensible as well as simple. This acronym may or may not be memorable because it has the same letters as the old one. So here is a new version that makes it clearer. It is longer and, of course, it presupposes that you can remember how to spell KITSCH, but it makes the point. In this one, the Sensible element is represented by the words Cool Headed, and the simplicity part is additionally emphasized by the adjective Terribly.

## KITSCH: Keep It Terribly Simple and Cool Headed

The *Terribly* element here forces you to be ruthless about the simplicity of the idea. If you can't express it in one or two sentences, it is probably too complicated. If your mate who doesn't know your industry can understand it, it is probably all right. It doesn't mean it is any good, but at least it's clear. Then comes the cool-headed part. There is no point in generating a head of steam about a new idea until you have worked it through properly. Passion is good. Enthusiasm is as well. But not if either are misdirected. If you let your heart run away with an idea before you have worked it out properly, you will waste your time and possibly your money.

> 'You do not really understand something unless you can explain it to your grandmother.'
>
> Albert Einstein

This approach is simple, but not simplistic. It means you are not allowed to wrap yourself up in incomprehensible words. No impenetrable jargon! No spreadsheets! Just a pen and plenty of paper, your preferred thinking conditions, and an appropriate chunk of time dedicated to the matter in hand. If you need a little help and stimulation to increase the chances of your having some decent ideas, there are hundreds of books dedicated to the subject. One of the best is *Flicking your Creative Switch* by Wayne Lotherington. Once again, if you don't have the time to get hold of a copy, there is a synopsis for you in the appendix. Don't say I don't look after you.

Here are some other enigmatic thoughts to help you along:

▶ Stand back and take a closer look.

▶ Death to compromise.

- ▶ Look before you reap.

- ▶ Other people's thoughts can't kill you, but your own could.

- ▶ Other people's thoughts can't kill you, but your own could keep you alive.

- ▶ Start with a bang, then bang again.

- ▶ Watch for shapes, then nip into the gaps.

- ▶ Ski off-piste for once.

- ▶ When the others zig, zag. Then zog.

One thing is for sure: it takes time and concentration, so don't think you can get away with a quick fix or a cursory skim over the issues. Muster all your mental energy and create the right conditions to allow your thoughts to flow properly.

> *'If a problem is hard, think, think, then think again. It will hurt at first, but you'll get used to it.'*
>
> Barbara Castle

**Unlock the facts: KITSCH**

Keep It Terribly Simple and Cool Headed. Don't overcomplicate what you do or how you explain it to people. Keep it simple, but not simplistic. And stay cool headed so you can make rational, constructive decisions.

# Didn't work? Try again

In his book *Outliers,* Malcolm Gladwell explains that Easterners have a stronger work ethic and so are better at maths because they are used to taking a lot of time to solve problems. This is the kind of tenacious attitude that you need to adopt when you are ensuring the survival of your business. If one piece of thinking or initiative doesn't work, then try another. And another. You are effectively testing each hypothesis in turn, like a good scientist, in an iterative process that allows you to learn as you go along. If you stop too early, you'll never know. As *Private Eye* notes: 'The scientific method consists of a researcher putting forward a new proposal and his or her colleagues testing the living daylights out of it without fear of the consequences.'

This takes tenacity, persistence, and an unswerving resolve that you will eventually get a result. So when you feel like stopping, keep going.

### Remember this: Try again

If something didn't work, then try again. The circumstances may well have changed: customer mood, economic factors, pricing, and hundreds of other details that might have had a bearing on it. Very few 'overnight successes' get it right first time.

> *'The mark of an educated mind is to be able to entertain an idea without accepting it.'*
>
> Aristotle

You have now pretty much completed your preparation for quality thinking. Be open-minded about what you come up with. Remember the Sensible element of the revised KISS principle. Adopt the attitude that 'if I try this, it might just work'. Consider the small stuff as well as the large, and steer clear of supposed big ideas and flabby management concepts that could distract you from the relevance of a clear, simple idea.

### Focus points

* Have you created the time to think?
* If so, when exactly, and for how long?
* Where are you going to do your thinking?
* How is this environment different from your normal one?
* Have you consulted any relevant books?
* Have you examined and dismissed distracting management concepts?
* Are you prepared to be open-minded?
* Are you ready to consider small things as well as large?
* How are you going to keep it simple?
* Are you genuinely prepared to try out the ideas you generate?

# Thinking stage 1: The facts

In this chapter you will learn:

- ► *How to establish the true facts about your business*
- ► *How to identify rivers and dams in your business*
- ► *How to apply common sense analysis*
- ► *To admit if something was a fluke*
- ► *Always to return to the original idea*

Stage 1 of the thinking process is based solely on the facts. At this point we are not interested in your opinion, or those of others. This is not because they are not valid or useful, but because they place an angle on the facts that will hinder us at first. So we are going to get the truth out on the table and examine it. This is what a client of mine used to call 'having the drains up'. If you find yourself fudging the answers, rip them up and start again. We do not want our thinking to suffer from factual pollution.

## Rivers and dams

First of all, imagine your business as a series of rivers and dams. These will be areas where everything is flowing well, or where there are frequently blockages that prevent you from conducting your business properly. Before you start, consider whether this process should be conducted on your own, or in the presence of others. If you are self-employed, or in charge of a company whose every workings are well known to you, then it might be a solo project. If not, it might be a suitable methodology for a brainstorm or away day. The latter will be appropriate if you are unaware of all the facts yourself. After you have read how the process works, revisit this point because once you have seen all the questions you will have a clearer idea of whether you are fully qualified to answer them all or not. The first step is to ask some questions and write down the answers.

Remember that rivers are things that flow well, and dams are places where they do not. We will start with the good stuff.

▶ Where are the rivers?

▶ How many of them are there?

▶ How large?

▶ How small?

▶ How many in total?

Put that to one side for a minute and take a deep breath. We are moving on to the not-so-good things.

- Where are the dams?

- How many of them are there?

- How large?

- How small?

- How many in total?

And put that list on the side. If it was a harrowing exercise, go for a walk or pour a stiff drink. Now answer the next question.

- Which do you have more of – rivers or dams?

This basic exercise should allow you to see at a glance what works in your business, and what doesn't. It will also reveal straightaway whether the business has more good things going on than bad, or vice versa. Don't panic at this stage if there seem to be way more dams than rivers. That's what we are here to sort out.

**Unlock the facts:** Rivers and dams

It's a simple enough analogy to work out what's good and bad in your business. What flows well and what causes blockages? Initiate more rivers and unblock the dams as fast as possible.

# Send it down to the boys in forensic or go completely ballistic?

The next step is examining the truth. I used to work with a guy who, whenever we received a written request from a client, would say: 'Send it down to the boys in forensic.' The gist of it was that we needed the full rundown on the subject matter and the task in hand before we could start pontificating about any possible solutions. He was right. These days, they call it strategic planning. Whatever you call it, it needs to be a great inquisition of all the available information. To get to the heart of the matter, it is worth looking at the definitions of forensic and forensics.

**Forensic** (*adjective*): relating to, or used in, a court of law

Forensic as an adjective means relating to, or used in a court of law. That means whatever it refers to must be solely concerned with the facts. Strangely though, the noun forensics refers to the study of formal debating, which is an opinion-based and non-factual pursuit.

**Forensics** (*noun*): the art or study of formal debating

So we are going to deploy a different, more scientific term to define the stage of our factual line of enquiry. The inspiration comes from the world of ballistics. Ballistics is only concerned with the facts, and at this stage, so are we. We are going to concentrate on the structural elements of your business, the tangible ones. Using the language of ballistics, we will divide the business into manageable chunks that we can then analyse.

**Ballistics** (*noun*): the study of the flight dynamics of projectiles; the interaction of the forces of propulsion, projectile aerodynamics, atmospheric resistance and gravity

Get out another clean sheet of paper and split it into five sections, each with a heading: projectiles, propulsion forces, aerodynamics, resistance and gravity. This is what the headings refer to:

▶ **Projectiles**: who, or what, is heading where?

▶ **Propulsion forces**: who, or what, is making them do that?

▶ **Aerodynamics**: who, or what, has good momentum behind it?

▶ **Resistance**: who, or what, is resisting forward motion?

▶ **Gravity**: is there anything structural that anchors any of this?

Don't fill in the headings at this stage. Put the piece of paper to one side. You might need it in a minute.

> *'Men occasionally stumble over the truth, but most of them pick themselves up and hurry off as if nothing happened.'*
> Winston Churchill

### Unlock the facts: Forensics and ballistics

Some people think they are gathering facts when they are merely rearranging their prejudices. If you are stuck in a rut, then make sure you use purely factual, near scientific ways of looking at your business. Don't let opinion come into it until you have the correct information.

## Common sense analysis

Now it is time to analyse what you've got. Stick to the facts and nothing else at this stage. We want the truth and nothing but. Don't ignore it. If you do, it will still be there tomorrow. Use your common sense. Common Sense Analysis is something I originally developed at university with my tutorial partner, Nick Middleton. There is no technique, other than using common sense – the sort that you would expect from a layperson in a pub. If there is a technique, it lies in the brutal simplicity of the questions, and the production of jargon-free answers. By now you should have roughly three piles of paper – one of rivers, one of dams, and one of ballistics. I say piles because you may be running a large, complicated business. If there is a lot of material, you might want to take a while to sort the wheat from the chaff and organize it into easily discernible parts.

### Remember this: Common sense analysis

If something seems nuts in your business, then apply a healthy dose of common sense. Every day we see examples of twisted thinking in the marketing of products. Don't allow nonsensical ideas to see the light of day.

Put the river information on the table and stare at it. Ask yourself this question:

▶ Why do these bits work so well?

Do not rush the answer(s). Write them down. Now apply some common sense analysis with more questions.

▶ Is that *really* the reason?

▶ Could it be for other reasons?

▶ If that is the reason, can I take it and apply it somewhere else in the business?

▶ Can I think of other possible applications?

From this process, you should be able to generate a highly promising list of ideas that emulate good things that your business already does. In other words, if something is a success, work out why and replicate it elsewhere. Some words of caution here though: always admit if something was a fluke.

Under no circumstances should you come away from this piece of analysis concluding that you should replicate something good elsewhere when you don't actually know why it worked in the first place. Sometimes, things just work through luck. Combinations of factors collide – timing, pricing, packaging, outside factors – to make something work, whether you planned them that way or not. If you were genuinely surprised by the success of something, and are not sure of the reasons behind that success, then admit it.

Do not go around pretending that you planned it all along – it will come back to bite you at some point. Just use the good thing to stimulate the next good thing. Use the principle: so that worked – have I got any more good ideas based on that?

Now put the dams on the table. This bit may be less pleasant, but it will be just as instructive. Ask yourself the question:

▶ Why do these bits not work well?

Write down the answers and again apply common sense analysis by probing with more questions.

- Is that *really* the reason?
- Could it be for other reasons?
- If so, what are they?
- If that is the reason, how can I fix it?
- If I can't fix it, who can?

If you can't see a clear way through it all, don't panic. Grab your ballistics sheet and review the headings.

- **Projectiles**: who, or what, is heading where?
- **Propulsion forces**: who, or what, is making them do that?
- **Aerodynamics**: who, or what, has good momentum behind it?
- **Resistance**: who, or what, is resisting forward motion?
- **Gravity**: is there anything structural that anchors any of this?

Now reorganize the rivers and dams information by the ballistics categories. Use the questions associated with each component to try to unravel how something might be resolved. For example, does a resistance question help solve an issue? Does the gravity of the business explain why something is as it is? Does a propulsion force provide a clue as to how to fix a dam? Here is a full set of examples.

### PROJECTILES
- Are we dealing with a projectile here?
- Who, or what, is heading where?
- Is that good or bad?
- If it's good, how can it be replicated elsewhere?
- If it's bad, how can it be fixed?

## PROPULSION FORCES

▶ Are we dealing with a propulsion force?

▶ Who, or what, is making them do that?

▶ Is that good or bad?

▶ If it's good, how can it be replicated elsewhere?

▶ If it's bad, how can it be fixed?

## AERODYNAMICS

▶ Is this to do with aerodynamics?

▶ Who, or what, has good momentum behind it?

▶ How can that be harnessed?

## RESISTANCE

▶ Is this a case of resistance?

▶ Who, or what, is resisting forward motion?

▶ How can that be fixed?

## GRAVITY

▶ Is gravity at work here?

▶ Is there something structural or cultural anchoring this?

▶ Can that be turned to our advantage or does it need fixing?

*'When the facts change, I change my mind. What do you do?'*
John Maynard Keynes

Hopefully, this type of cross-examination should be helping to shed any fuzzy thinking. Remember we are still only dealing in the realms of fact. It is your job to face the facts maturely, and see them for what they are. Do not let bias and prejudice creep in to your thinking, and be prepared to change your mind if the facts suggest that it would be a good idea to do so.

*'The more you learn the worse things get.'*

Mark Twain

There may be a certain element here of not wanting to face the truth, but you must. Take heart from the fact that all intelligent people and successful businesses learn from mistakes. This is the very essence of all successful evolution. If you are not capable of working out what went wrong and how it could be done better next time, then your business will never evolve. So be reassured that making mistakes is perfectly fine, so long as you are able to identify them accurately, and then take the necessary remedial action.

*'Mistakes are the portals of discovery.'*

James Joyce

It was once said that we all make mistakes, and when we have made enough, they call it experience. Do not be afraid of mistakes. They usually lead to something else, particularly if they are absorbed humbly and thoughtfully. Another way of looking at it is that you can't make any mistakes if you don't do anything, and vice versa. If you never cook, you never spill any ingredients on the floor. If you never wash up, you never break any plates. Some form of action with a few flaws is far preferable to inaction.

*'The man who makes no mistakes does not usually make anything.'*

Edward John Phelps

*'I've learnt from my mistakes, and I'm sure I can repeat them.'*

Peter Cook

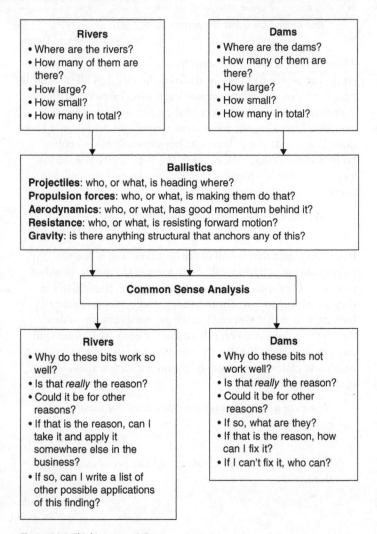

**Figure 14.1** Thinking stage 1: Facts

Also be aware that you need to approach your thinking with the right tools for the job. If an issue is highly technical, then you may wish to use this process alongside someone who knows the technical detail, and can therefore answer the majority of the tricky questions that it throws up. There's no point in generating scores of questions that you cannot personally answer, unless it is your specific intent to raise them all, and then go to the experts for their solutions. Far better to embark on the process with an approximate idea of what you think might emerge, and have the necessary people on hand to help you out.

> *'If all you have is a hammer, everything begins to look like a nail.'*
>
> Nietzsche

Diving in to any wide-ranging thought process without decent preparation is inadvisable. If you embark on it with only one angle, you may only generate the one solution, and it will probably be the same as everything you have come up with before. Most issues have multiple possible solutions, so you need to stay open-minded as to what these might be. This may mean that, if you adopt this thinking technique, you might want to run it in parallel with another method to see if you emerge with a richer combination of ideas and answers.

> *'When you have a hammer all problems start to look like a nail. But when you don't have a hammer, you don't want anything to look like a nail.'*
>
> Robert Kagan

I guess Nietzsche made his observation long before Robert Kagan, but his addition to the analogy makes an interesting point. If you embark on some careful thought without any techniques or any shape to organize your thinking, then you may well only emerge with a re-statement of your problems. So try to regard this technique as your hammer, and hit those nails right on the head.

## Always admit if something was a fluke

A quick word of warning about the positive things that fall into the rivers category. Do not be tempted to claim that these things were wonderfully devised and thought through if, in truth, they were actually a fluke. Only you know the reality of this. If you allow this fuzzy thinking to happen, then you will assume that their success will be replicated if you repeat them, but you will simply be throwing your business open to random forces of chance. So don't do it. Have the maturity to accept that it was a fluke, and don't build your next move on a fallacy of the past.

### Try it now: Was it a fluke?

When looking back at successes in your business and looking for inspiration, always admit if something was a fluke. Far too many people (and businesses) rewrite history to claim that a random success was carefully thought through. Most are not, so don't fool yourself.

# Remind me, what *was* the original idea?

One final point on the Facts stage: if you find yourself getting in a muddle, do stop and ask yourself this fundamental question: What *was* the original idea? It could refer to anything – why you set the business up in the first place, what the vision or purpose of your company is, why you bother to come to work in the morning – anything that is crucial to the matter in hand.

### Unlock the facts: The original idea

After you have been running your business for a while it is very easy to forget why you set it up in the first place. If things are drifting, take the time to remind yourself of the original point.

### Focus points

* Have you written out your lists of rivers and dams?
* Did you analyse them carefully to find out why things are as they are?
* What did you conclude?
* Did you try the ballistic questions?
* What did that reveal?
* Did you look at your successes to see if they were flukes?
* Have you worked out how to replicate good things elsewhere?
* Have you revisited your original idea for the business?
* How are you going to fix the bad bits?
* What was the mistake you learnt most from and why?

# 15

# Thinking stage 2: Your own opinion

In this chapter you will learn:

- ► *How to harness your own opinion*
- ► *How to heed your own counsel*
- ► *The drawbacks of not doing so*
- ► *The difference between scepticism and cynicism*
- ► *How to be pragmatic, but not to compromise*

# The doctor who died of ill health

So you have the facts on the table in front of you. What works, and what doesn't. Now is the time to introduce your opinion to the equation. You will be familiar with the phrase: heed your own counsel. And yet life is full of examples of people who fail to do precisely that. Whether it is true or not, received wisdom suggests that doctors always tell you how to live longer, that smoking is bad, and that you need to improve your fitness and your diet. But do they practise what they preach? Frequently not. Decorators often have tatty houses that need a lick of paint. They don't want to come home and do for themselves what they do all day for a living. And advertising agencies are often poor at promoting themselves, despite the fact that they do it successfully every day for their clients.

So the point is, you give out good advice all day – are you capable of paying attention to your own advice? This is what this section is all about: heeding your own counsel, and listening to your own opinion.

> **Opinion** (*noun*): judgement or belief not founded on certainty or proof

The facts will, in the main, speak for themselves, and the nasty home truths certainly will, so don't dwell on those. Now start considering what your perspective on the issues is. If you are conducting this process as part of a strategic rethink with colleagues, then you might want to get them to contribute their opinions too. Just make sure that people don't all dive in with their opinions and prejudices at the beginning. Make sure that stage 1 has been done first. Then you can evaluate their opinions in the context of the facts, rather than just as a random series of views.

> *'Don't argue for the difficulties. The difficulties will argue for themselves.'*
>
> Winston Churchill

In the next chapter, we will scrutinize the opinions of 60 or more business people, and one of the recurring themes is that you should always trust your instincts. Up until the mid-1980s, it was normal for people in business to have a hunch and go with it. Then came research, pre-testing, and a range of other techniques for checking if an idea was viable before it ever saw the light of day. For enormous product launches that require multi-million pound investments, that is totally valid. But for simple, ingenious ways of galvanizing your business, it is totally unnecessary. Have a hunch and go for it. If it doesn't work, do something else. In another Malcolm Gladwell book, *Blink*, he explains how a snap judgement made very quickly can actually be more effective than one made deliberately and cautiously. He introduces the notion of thin slicing, in which the impression gained of something in the first two seconds is almost always more reliable than one built up over a longer period of time.

So trust your instincts, and those of respected colleagues. Do not ignore your own counsel and become a doctor who dies of ill health, having failed to listen to your own advice. We will start by dragging your opinions out of you, and then go on to introduce some devil's advocate elements to test-drive those opinions for validity.

### Unlock the facts: The dead doctor

It always seems odd when your doctor tells you that smoking will kill you when he smokes himself. Don't be that doctor. Apply all your experience to your business and practise what you preach.

## Heed your own counsel

Take your sheets of rivers, dams and ballistics, and re-read them. Work through each in turn, asking yourself these questions. Remember to heed your own counsel.

▶ What do I *personally* think of this issue?

▶ What does my colleague think?

▶ If it's a bad thing, do I know how to fix it?

- ▶ If it's a good thing, how can I develop it?
- ▶ What is my immediate thought about what to do next?

Write down the answers to these and put them on one side. Now start making some decisions. If an idea is rubbish, throw it away. By now, some of the ideas will have bitten the dust, and those that remain on the table are probably pretty robust. Review what is left and, if necessary, write them out again because they may have taken a bit of a battering on the way. It is worthwhile taking the time to do this because scribbled ideas with too many comments on them are often confusing. Ideally, an idea should consist of one word or one sentence. If expressed that simply, it is much easier to determine whether it is going to work or not. Only ever put one idea on one piece of paper, so as not to confuse or interlink any of them. Chuck away all the old scribbles and go off and do something different. If you have been at it for a while, take a breather or come back to it tomorrow. So, to recap, you should now have just one pile of paper, each with one idea on it, expressed either as one sentence or, better still, one word.

**Remember this:** Heed your own counsel

If you possibly can, ask yourself what the most sensible view of your business is, and apply that straightaway. If you find it hard to be objective, then ask a trusted friend, colleague or adviser and listen carefully to what they say.

# The pragmatist who was sceptical about the cynic

Now we are going to introduce the devil's advocate, or the devil's avocado as an old colleague always used to say. As you know, that is an opposing, and often unpopular, view and in business these can take various forms. For this part of the thinking process, I have chosen two views: sceptical and cynical.

Once we have examined these in detail, we will counterbalance them with a healthy dose of pragmatism.

Let's start at the sharp end. A cynic is someone who thinks the worst of almost every person or situation. At their most extreme, they are no fun to have around. Sometimes they are called killers, because they only ever kill ideas and they never seem to have any themselves.

**Cynic** (*noun*): a person who believes the worst about people or the outcome of events

As a personality trait, therefore, cynicism is not very desirable, but as an aid to rational thought, it can be very helpful in sorting out which ideas are good and which are lousy. Hundreds of years ago, a cynic was a member of a sect founded by a guy called Antisthenes. These people scorned worldly things and believed that self-control was the key to the only good available in the world. A pretty heavy notion I'm sure you'll agree, but that's by the by. For our purposes, a short, sharp blast of cynicism will sort the wheat from the chaff, the good ideas from the not-so-good. As the saying goes, the good is the enemy of the great. In fact, some people are active fans of cynicism, and believe it is as close as you can get to truly accurate observation.

*'The power of accurate observation is often called cynicism by those who do not have it.'*

George Bernard Shaw

So we are going to cross-examine our ideas with a set of cynical questions. You might think that this approach is a bit strange, but there is a method behind the madness. You have probably come across Edward de Bono's system of putting on different coloured hats to represent different character types and ways of thinking. Well, this is similar, but you can do it on your own. It forces you to adopt frames of mind that you wouldn't usually consider if left to your own devices and, crucially, it enables you to replicate the possible reactions of colleagues and customers to the new ideas. So the next part of this stage is to ask a series of cynical questions. Here we go.

- What's the point of that?

- That will never work, will it?

- That didn't work before so it won't work now, will it?

- They'll never go for that, will they?

- How can we afford that?

- No one is going to buy that, are they?

I haven't gone on and on with a long list, because the negative nature of these questions is quite draining. Don't overdo it. Just briefly adopt the position of someone who cannot see a way through for the proposed idea. It will rapidly reveal whether the initiative can withstand aggressive scrutiny.

Now we are going to move on to a milder line of enquiry, basing it on scepticism. Originally a sceptic was a member of one of the ancient Greek schools of philosophy, populated by people like Pyrrho, who believed that real knowledge of things is impossible. Another rather weighty philosophical thought, but again, not one that should put us off much. Sceptics aren't saying no to something, they just aren't convinced. What they want is more proof that something is likely to work.

There is a lovely moment in a book called *The Pirate Inside* by Adam Morgan where he describes the personal characteristics that make individuals in companies agitate for change. When interviewing Bob Gill of Pringles, he asks him what his reaction is whenever someone says no to an idea. 'Oh,' he says, 'you basically treat the word no as a request for further information.' How brilliant is that? Ever the optimist, lively bright people in business believe so much in their ideas that they just keep going until everybody else says yes. So consider this sceptical element of the thinking process as a request for further verification that the idea in question does indeed have merit.

> **Sceptical** (*adjective*): not convinced that something is true; tending to mistrust people and ideas

Go back to your pile of ideas, and subject them to some further interrogation.

▶ How will that work then?

▶ Will it be viable?

▶ Will people be impressed by it?

▶ Will it complement the current business well?

▶ Can the idea be pushed even further?

▶ Are there even more possibilities beyond that?

It doesn't matter in what order you ask these questions, nor whether you ask the cynical set before or after this sceptical set. The important thing is that you have embarked on some form of elimination process. This will ensure that you don't waste time later pursuing ideas when you could already have worked out for yourself that they probably wouldn't work anyway.

> 'If one regards oneself as a sceptic, it is as well from time to time to be sceptical about one's scepticism.'
>
> Freud

Round three takes the pragmatist's perspective. This is where we survey the two extreme sets of opinions and draw them together to strike some sort of sensible balance. This is not the same as killing a perfectly good idea. It is sense-checking the likelihood of something actually getting done.

**Pragmatism** (*noun*): the doctrine that the content of a concept consists only in its practical applicability

An idea is only as good as your ability to enact it, so what we now need is a pragmatic check. Review the ideas asking these questions.

▶ Can you afford it?

▶ Have you got the resources to implement it?

▶ Will customers and colleagues accept it?

▶ Have you got the time to do it?

For more than 200 questions on whether something can truly be done, read *So What?*

**Remember this: Pragmatist, sceptic or cynic?**

You need to be able to adopt all three roles to come to a balanced view about your business. The sceptic asks if an idea is truly feasible. The cynic says it will never work (a good pressure test). And the pragmatist works out whether it is worth it and how it can be done.

# Death to compromise

You should be down to a highly manageable number by now, so all that is left is a reality check and some fine-tuning. Pause for a minute or, as a colleague of mine used to say, stand back and take a closer look. This is the point at which you need to agree if you are happy to go public with the ideas. There is no room for compromise here. You are either going to do it, or you are not.

▶ Is there any element of bluff or self-delusion in it?

▶ Is it a forced fit or does it sit comfortably with everything else?

▶ Could it be better articulated?

▶ Is it free of jargon?

▶ Can you relate to it?

▶ Will other people?

▶ Are you happy to go public with it?

> **Compromise** (*noun*): settlement by concessions on both sides; something midway between two or more different things

That's pretty much it. Just don't compromise the idea or how you are going to execute it. Remember: you are either going to do it, or you are not. Be decisive, and get ready to enact it.

**Remember this:** Death to compromise

Once you have thought about something carefully and decided to do it,
don't do it half-heartedly. Do it properly, give it your best shot, and don't
cut corners.

> 'Consensus is when we have a discussion. They tell me
> what they think. Then I decide.'
>
> Lee Iacocca

**Try it now:** Trust your instincts

As a final guide to decision-making, trust your own instincts. Studies
suggest that this will be accurate and helpful about 80 per cent of
the time. So if it feels right, then do it. You can always change your
mind later.

This chapter was all about coming to decisions. You have
covered a lot of ground now, so it is time to pause and
reflect. You should have taken the facts, and overlaid your
own opinion. If that was a bit wishy-washy in places, the
cynical or sceptical view should have helped to crystallize
your opinion, so that you could reach a consensus with
yourself. You should have ended up with one clear pile of
ideas, rigorously sense-checked for their practicability. In a
way, therefore, you are ready to enact them, and if you feel
completely confident in them, then do go ahead and do that
now. If you are still anxious, discuss them with a colleague.
If you don't have anyone of that type, or even if you would
value a second opinion, you might want to look at the next
chapter. It contains a vast amount of other people's wisdom.

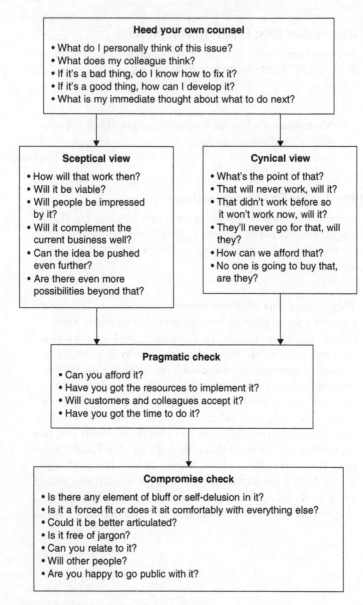

**Heed your own counsel**

- What do I personally think of this issue?
- What does my colleague think?
- If it's a bad thing, do I know how to fix it?
- If it's a good thing, how can I develop it?
- What is my immediate thought about what to do next?

**Sceptical view**

- How will that work then?
- Will it be viable?
- Will people be impressed by it?
- Will it complement the current business well?
- Can the idea be pushed even further?
- Are there even more possibilities beyond that?

**Cynical view**

- What's the point of that?
- That will never work, will it?
- That didn't work before so it won't work now, will it?
- They'll never go for that, will they?
- How can we afford that?
- No one is going to buy that, are they?

**Pragmatic check**

- Can you afford it?
- Have you got the resources to implement it?
- Will customers and colleagues accept it?
- Have you got the time to do it?

**Compromise check**

- Is there any element of bluff or self-delusion in it?
- Is it a forced fit or does it sit comfortably with everything else?
- Could it be better articulated?
- Is it free of jargon?
- Can you relate to it?
- Will other people?
- Are you happy to go public with it?

**Figure 15.1** Thinking stage 2: Your own opinion

## Focus points

* ✳ Have you heeded your own counsel?
* ✳ Have you trusted your instincts?
* ✳ Did you adopt the cynical position?
* ✳ Did that force you to reject some ideas?
* ✳ Did you pose the sceptical questions?
* ✳ Have you overcome those reservations or clarified things as a result?
* ✳ What did the pragmatic check reveal?
* ✳ Have you compromised at all in any of this?
* ✳ Are you ready to go public with the ideas?
* ✳ Have you paused to reflect on progress so far?

# 16

# Thinking stage 3: The experience of others

In this chapter you will learn:

▶ *Other people's answers to six fascinating questions*

▶ *How you can apply them to your own business*

Stage 3 of the thinking process is drawing upon the experience and wisdom of others. This is not so much a process as a bit of osmosis. All business people are fascinated by the experiences of others, so here we collect a wide range of opinions and try to organize them in such a way as to help you develop your own business. This is very much a do-it-yourself chapter. If you are particularly interested in one question, go straight to it to see the answers.

## The survey explained

The survey asked 60 people running their own businesses six questions:

1  What is the hardest thing about running and growing your business?

2  Is growth always a good thing?

3  Did you ever suffer from post-launch blues or a three-year itch?

4  How do you plan the 'next big thing'?

5  If you could have known one thing when you started that you know now, what would it be?

6  Is there anything else you would like to pass on about growing or evolving your business?

Here are their answers and suggested approaches.

# Question 1: What is the hardest thing about running and growing your business?

▶ Have a clear understanding of why your business exists.

▶ Work hard on motivation.

▶ Be patient.

▶ Keep a close eye on time pressures.

▶ Nurture contacts carefully.

▶ Take the plunge and take risks.

- Learn to let go of some things.
- Use your partners judiciously.
- Find brave customers.
- Grow prudently.
- Keep an eye on escalating bureaucracy.
- Spend the time to find the right people and build the right team.
- Remember different skills are required to set up a business than to grow one.
- You don't have to win by much to win by a lot.
- Save today's income for tomorrow's expansion.
- Avoid going after everything that moves.
- Only acquire businesses to add skill sets you do not already have.
- Find the time to invest in growth.
- If you're not an interesting person, people won't want to do business with you.

**Remember this:** Approaching growth

You need to get in the right frame of mind. If you aim for growth, you will probably survive. If you aim only for survival, you may struggle. It's not about being hopelessly optimistic. It's about having lots of ideas and initiatives so that you can afford to fail on a fair proportion of them.

# Question 2: Is growth always a good thing?

- To stay as you are is impossible.
- Momentum is important but size in itself is not.
- Adopt a mentality of growth.
- There is good growth and bad growth.

- Bad growth is doing things for the wrong reasons.

- Growth is good so long as it is profitable.

- Growth usually involves making a lot of mistakes.

- Work out how much money you want to extract and over what time period.

- Make sure quality of service is maintained.

- Do not pursue growth for growth's sake.

- Be careful to manage, control and plan your growth.

- Top up your leaky bucket constantly.

- Differentiate between higher turnover and better margin.

- Rapid growth can endanger quality and reputation.

- Know when to turn down business.

- A principle isn't a principle until it costs you money.

- Turnover or revenue is vanity, profit is sanity.

- Do not compromise what you set out to achieve in the first place.

- Don't change the thing that most clients like.

- Don't grow too fast and dilute what enabled you to grow in the first place.

- Avoid being 'medium'.

# Question 3: Did you ever suffer from post-launch blues or a three-year itch?

- Regard a launch as the beginning of the beginning rather than the end of the beginning.

- Tell yourself in advance that the honeymoon period will end.

- Continually question what your business does and how well it does it.

- Keep transforming it into a shinier, newer version of itself.

- Entrepreneurs are often good 'starters' or 'creators' but poor at routine.
- Work out how to deal with the highs and lows.
- Give yourself credit for what you have already achieved.
- Remind yourself why you're doing it.
- Look around and compare with worse options.
- You and your partners have to evolve along with your business.
- Remember that most people in business have itchy and low times.
- Be aware that partners get the blues too, so act sensitively.
- Have the idea, build the car, then employ someone else to drive it for you.
- Realize that the business will never be 'finished'.
- Launching a business is a bit like having a baby.
- Running it can be like the loneliness of the long-distance runner.
- Get a good non-exec to offer a different, less emotional perspective.

### Try it now: Blues and itches

Everybody has low times. Sometimes these are operational or financial, but more frequently they are motivational. It's natural and human. So don't beat yourself up if you get the blues or an itch to do something else. Use the emotion as a springboard for sensible reflection, and then decide what you are going to do about it.

# Question 4: How do you plan the 'next big thing'?

- Have an idea where you want to go but always be open to other opportunities.
- Talk to people who know more about it than you do and hear about their lives.

- Make quick decisions about opportunities that could influence your growth.

- Go for a long walk or a run, or take a shower for inspiration.

- You only need to be five minutes ahead of the pack to succeed.

- Keep your big picture clear and at the forefront of everything you do.

- Ask your team.

- Keep lifting your head up and be ready to take opportunities.

- Always have a pen and paper handy.

- Make time for planning.

- Reinvent your business all the time.

- Listen to your customers and bright people.

- Look how successful businesses manage expansion in other sectors.

- Listen to what is happening around you.

- Allow yourself the time away to contemplate 'what else?'

- Start with the people and the casting.

- Have an annual day of reflection.

- Be spurred on by ambitions that are way beyond your current reach.

- Get away from the business to have enlightening moments of inspiration.

- Use external consultants or facilitators to move into novel related areas.

### Remember this: The 'next big thing'

Your next move may indeed be relatively big. If so, well done, you have clearly worked it all out carefully. Much more frequently however, you will have lots of little ideas. In total, these can be just as important as that elusive big thing, so pursue them with just as much vigour and keep them coming.

# Question 5: If you could have known one thing when you started that you know now, what would it be?

► Plan and test everything before you set up.

► Be confident and have a clear picture of your worth.

► Equity is forever. Be very careful to whom you give equity.

► Everything takes a lot longer than you think.

► Make sure you're prepared for the rollercoaster ride.

► Networking is essential as talent alone in some cases is not enough.

► Invest in friendships and relationships – the rest will happen naturally.

► Understand the selling points which trigger income-generating responses.

► Listen to your gut feeling – it's usually right.

► All businesses are people businesses.

► Everyone running a business goes through some big lows.

► Few other people are as excited by your business or as committed as you are.

► Your customers know less about your subject matter than you do.

► Business is not personal.

► Your first instincts are normally right.

► Everything is negotiable.

► It is always about people, people, people.

► Always act and tell the truth fast.

► Talented craftspeople are by no means talented managers.

► Don't keep pursuing something if it isn't a success.

► If you don't do it, you don't get paid.

# Question 6: Is there anything else you would like to pass on about growing or evolving your business?

▶ You have to love what you do.

▶ Be absolutely clear about what your product or service is.

▶ Greed is usually transparent.

▶ You're probably better than you think you are – don't sell yourself too cheap.

▶ There are some people it's just not worth trying with.

▶ Enjoy the process of building the business, not just the dream of what you will one day achieve.

▶ Be brave, say what you really think, and go to bed knowing you did your best.

▶ Make mistakes and learn.

▶ Don't be afraid to move on from something if it is not working.

▶ Be with the people you enjoy being with.

▶ Reputation in any market is worth more than anything else.

▶ Never be afraid to ask advice from someone you admire.

▶ Do the important things first – don't put them off.

▶ Treat all people as you would expect to be treated yourself.

▶ Believe in what you are doing and at the same time listen to healthy criticism.

- ▶ Past success doesn't mean future success.
- ▶ Reach for the stars.

**Try it now: Pass it on**

If you are in the fortunate position of having gained a lot of experience of surviving in business, then have the generosity of spirit to pass that on to someone else. It's an unwritten rule amongst small business owners that they help each other out. So if you have helpful advice, pass it on.

# Whole survey diagnosis

Of course, there are some contradictory comments, but a theme running through it all is the value of paying attention to the experiences of others, and to experts such as non-executive directors and outside advisers who are less emotionally attached to the business. Beware the casual adviser or the quick fix, don't cut corners and arrive in the wrong place, and bear in mind cheap advice can often be the most expensive.

One other theme I think is worth commenting on. Growth can become more important the larger your company gets. In the main, sole traders, partnerships and companies with fewer than ten staff are quite apprehensive about growth, and more interested in sensible survival and reasonable profits. Those with several hundred employees think it is pretty much essential to retain momentum, or to placate shareholders. This is not statistically verifiable, but the sway of opinion is that anxieties about growth are more acute the more people you have – something of an irony.

With regard to the thinking method, you have now finished stage three. Stage one gathered the facts, stage two added your own opinion, and now you have seen the opinions and experiences of others. There is only one remaining question you need to ask yourself about what you have read in this chapter:

- ▶ What can I learn from what other people have been through?

Take your list of ideas and consider them in the context of all the advice here. If anything has touched a particular nerve in relation to your business, then have a think and make the necessary changes. You have now finished the thinking process.

## Focus points

- ✲ Do you have a clear understanding of why your business exists?
- ✲ Are you learning to let go of some things?
- ✲ Do you use your partners judiciously?
- ✲ Are you keeping an eye on escalating bureaucracy?
- ✲ Do you continually question what your business does and how well it does it?
- ✲ Do you keep transforming it into a shinier, newer version of itself?
- ✲ Do you realize that the business will never be 'finished'?
- ✲ Are you listening to what is happening around you?
- ✲ Can you allow yourself the time away to contemplate 'what else?'
- ✲ Do you understand the selling points that trigger income-generating responses?

# 17

# Setting up tripwires and grenades

In this chapter you will learn:

▶ *How to trip yourself up on purpose*
▶ *How to set up idea, personal and business tripwires*
▶ *How to detonate idea, personal and business grenades*
▶ *The value of rapid sequential tasking*
▶ *How to put the effort in only where it gets you somewhere*

# How to trip yourself up on purpose

So you have done a lot of thinking, and now is the time to decide how precisely you are going to implement the great ideas you have generated. We don't want them languishing on a piece of paper in a drawer somewhere and never seeing the light of day. Getting them done will require a mixture of business effort and personal effort, and in this chapter we are going to deal with the business perspective. It is all about setting up your business tripwires so that you cannot fail to action something. Many of us know that if we don't write something down, we will most likely forget it. That could be a sticky note on the back of the door saying 'don't forget keys', a shopping list, or a note on the steering wheel saying 'oil' or 'petrol'.

Whatever the task, if you write it down and put it in the right place, it becomes impossible to forget the important thing when the time comes. This is the principle behind business tripwires. We are going to work out what will go wrong *before* it does, and put the measures in place to prevent that from happening. To make this really effective, you need to have the drains up and work out how everything works, and work out where it is most likely to fall down. Predict that, and you will ensure that the important things truly get done.

> *'If you're going to do something, go start. Life's simpler than we sometimes can admit.'*
>
> Robert De Niro

# Write it down and it gets done

Discussing broad concepts in their embryonic phase can be fun, particularly for those who don't have to get the thing in question done. But nothing irritates a decent businessperson more than a good idea that hasn't quite seen the light of day. No one cares why – the point is, it is still on the drawing board and the fruits of it have not been realized.

Often this is because there is confusion about whose responsibility it actually is. Other times it is because the idea is allowed to drift and no one pushes for any particular deadline to be met. The trick is to write it down. As Robert De Niro says, if you intend to start, then start. It's that simple. The precise list of what needs to be done will depend on which ideas you have come up with and what matters most to your business, but we will start with some likely subjects, and you can customize the system to reflect your own circumstances. Here are some examples of idea tripwires.

**Remember this:** Trip yourself up

It doesn't sound very helpful, but it is. If you know you are not very good at something, or are likely to forget to do it, then do something now to anticipate that difficulty and thus increase your effectiveness when the time comes.

## Idea tripwires

▶ How is this idea going to get done?

▶ Who is going to do it?

▶ By when?

Repeat this process for every idea. If the answer to any question is longer than one word, be suspicious of it. If it is longer than a sentence, it won't get done, so try again. If the answer to the second question is you, then write reminders in your personal organizer now to make sure it gets done. If the answer is someone other than you, get them to agree that they will, and put the same tripwires in their organizer. The date by which it gets done needs careful thought. If you can trust yourself to meet a deadline, then great.

If you can't, then put the necessary reminders in the way before it becomes time critical, and set yourself sanctions for missing your own timings. Don't fudge this. In his book

*Simply Brilliant,* Fergus O'Connell points out that things either are or they aren't. In other words, they are either done or not done. So don't console yourself with unhelpful thoughts such as 'I'm halfway through it' or 'It's all in hand'. It is either finished, and ready to go public, or it isn't, and if it isn't, it's either late or useless. If you want to know more about this clear way of thinking, there is a summary of the book in the appendix.

'To *undertake* is to achieve.'

Emily Dickinson

Now set up your tripwires by getting up close and personal. Answer these questions and, crucially, enact right now the thing that will make sure it happens.

# Personal planning tripwires

▶ What will make me get this done?

▶ Is that bulletproof, or too flimsy?

▶ Does that allow me to wriggle out of it later?

▶ If so, what sanction will force me to do it?

▶ Have I actually put that in place right now?

There is no room for excuses here because it is completely in your interests to get the thing done, even if it does lie a little way in the future. This technique works for specific items, but it also works for the overall shape of your business. If this is an exercise that you would find useful, then you might want to write down your one-year, three-year, five-year and ten-year aims. Actually, the time spans don't matter, but the principle does. Choose frequencies that are appropriate to your business, and write down the answers to these questions.

# Business planning tripwires

▶ What, ultimately, do I want for my business?

▶ By when?

▶ How exactly am I going to get there?

▶ Do I need help, and if so, from whom?

▶ Have I started yet?

> *'The beginning is half of every action.'*
>
> Greek proverb

Whoever the Greek person was, they had it right. The world is full of people who claim to have lots of ideas but, strangely, haven't quite started them. Do not allow yourself to be one of these people. Get started immediately, and learn as you go. You can always change your plan on the way, but don't fall into the trap of standing around pontificating when you could be using the time to get the thing done.

 **Try it now:** Tripwires

Design your tripwires now to improve all aspects of your business. Put them in place to generate better ideas, and to plan your business and personal lives better.

# Dropping grenades in fishponds

There is another technique that works for some people who need constant reminders to get organized and get stuff done. I call it dropping grenades in fishponds. The idea here is that you deliberately create cataclysmic circumstances in order to jolt yourself into doing the necessary thing. Some people need a severe shock to force them to do something, so here is a form of disaster planning that may help catapult you into action. We will call them grenades.

**Cataclysm** (*noun*): violent upheaval

---

**Idea tripwires**

- How is this idea going to get done?
- Who is going to do it?
- By when?

---

**Personal planning tripwires**

- What will make me get this done?
- Is that bulletproof, or too flimsy?
- Does that allow me to wriggle out of it later?
- If so, what sanction will force me to do it?
- Have I actually put that in place right now?

---

**Business planning tripwires**

- What, ultimately, do I want for my business?
- By when?
- How exactly am I going to get there?
- Do I need help, and if so, from whom?
- Have I started yet?

---

**Figure 17.1** Tripwires checklist.

The purpose of these questions is not to scare you senseless and prevent you from sleeping well. It is to scare up the important issues for those who bumble along for too long without actually getting done the bits that they know in their hearts will really make a difference.

# Idea grenades

▶ What if this were the only idea available?

▶ What if it never happened?

▶ What if there were 20 more like this?

You can see how this extreme line of questioning pushes everything that bit further. Go a bit over the top to test your mettle. If this were the only idea you had, would you still do it? There's no point in wasting time on tripwires and implementation if you aren't convinced, and if you aren't, then why should your colleagues or customers be?

# Personal grenades

▶ What if I could never work again?

▶ What if I took a year off?

▶ What if I quit this and did something totally different?

These are pretty poignant too, and the intention is to make you stop and think so that you can work out the severity of an item and how badly you want to do it. Then, if you conclude that it definitely does matter, you can engineer the necessary tripwires. We will investigate all this further in the next chapter when you write your Lifesmile Statement.

# Business grenades

▶ What if the business folded tomorrow?

▶ What if all the staff were fired?

▶ What if all our customers suddenly disappeared?

Nasty scorched earth scenarios like this are very polarizing and are good for helping you to clarify your thoughts so that you really know what you are trying to achieve. The principle is the same as for your personal issues. Use this Armageddon approach to determine how badly something matters, and how you are going to guarantee that it gets done.

## Unlock the facts: Grenades

Explosive ideas have the power to turbo-charge your business. But they don't occur all by themselves. You need to engineer time and space to invent clever interventions that will ignite your business.

► **Idea grenades**

► What if this were the only idea available?

► What if it never happened?

► What if there were 20 more like this?

► **Personal grenades**

► What if I could never work again?

► What if I took a year off?

► What if I quit this and did something totally different?

► **Business grenades**

► What if the business folded tomorrow?

► What if all the staff were fired?

► What if all our customers suddenly disappeared?

**Idea grenades**

- What if this were the only idea available?
- What if it never happened?
- What if there were 20 more like this?

**Personal grenades**

- What if I could never work again?
- What if I took a year off?
- What if I quit this and did something totally different?

**Business grenades**

- What if the business folded tomorrow?
- What if all the staff were fired?
- What if all our cutomers suddenly disappeared?

**Figure 17.2** Grenades checklist.

# Don't replace the original, replace the spare

We are working on the principle here that small reminders yield big results. It just depends how severe a memory jog you require, and only you can be the judge of that. If you are quite efficient, then you may not need any of these measures at all. If you have trouble with motivation, or you are a bit disorganized, then you may well do. Put the appropriate number of tripwires in place, but don't overdo it to the point that they are constantly preventing you from doing the task in hand. They are there to make you do things, not to stop you from doing them. If you put too many in place, you will be damming up the river to see how it flows, which would be pointless. Or, put another way, pulling the flowers up to see how they grow.

But there are also simple principles you can apply that save prevarication in your working day, week or year. One of my favourites is 'don't replace the original, replace the spare'. Every good chef knows that you need a spare of everything, so that when you run out of the original, you simply reach for it, and the meal still happens. Many people in life never have a spare, so whenever they run out of something there is a panic. They then either rush about in a mad flap to buy another item, thus increasing their stress, or the meal doesn't happen. The analogy applies equally to those in business. Whether it is supplies or human resource, you always need a spare. When the spare is used up, buy another spare. Don't replace the original, replace the spare.

# Multitasking versus Rapid Sequential Tasking

Part of the knack of making sure things get done is realizing what you are actually capable of doing. Getting a lot done is often associated with multitasking, and there has been a lot of discussion about whether everyone is able to do it.

**Multitask** (*verb*): to work at several different tasks simultaneously

One theory suggests that women are far better at multitasking than men, and the evidence for that looks quite convincing. So if you are male and no good at multitasking, what can you do? My suggestion is Rapid Sequential Tasking. If you can only do one thing at a time, then do it fast and move on to the next thing. Everyone has checklists, and they usually contain a curious mixture of important and trivial things to do. My research in scores of training sessions suggests that the average number of items on a checklist is between seven and twenty. If it is less than seven, there is no need for a list, and if it is longer than twenty, then the list is too demoralizing so the small things aren't added to it. So strip out the easy trivia from the important stuff, and rattle through it sequentially and quickly. Just because guys apparently can't 'do' multitasking, it doesn't mean they can't do Rapid Sequential Tasking.

 **Try it now: Multitasking v Rapid Sequential Tasking**

If you can't cope with doing everything at once, then consider doing things in a sequence. Even one in a row is good. Do simple tasks first and fast, and liberate proper time for more complex tasks.

# Put the effort in only where it gets you somewhere

Your ability to get stuff done is one thing. Whether you are doing the right stuff in the first place is a completely different matter. Any good businessperson will tell you that you need to develop the knack of working out whether you are pursuing the right opportunities, and deciding how much time and effort to spend on them. One of the hardest decisions to make is to pull out of something when you have invested a lot of physical and emotional energy into it. But pull out is precisely what you must do if the thing in question is going nowhere.

> *'If at first you don't succeed, try, try again. Then give up. No use being a damn fool about it.'*
>
> W. C. Fields

Try again by all means, and again. But don't keep repeating the same mistakes or misjudgements.

> *'The definition of insanity is doing the same thing over and over again and expecting different results.'*
>
> Benjamin Franklin

You require a level of tenacity to get something done, and good judgement to decide when to retire gracefully. W. C. Fields suggests a fair bit of tenacity, coupled with the good sense to give up eventually when you have got nowhere.

> *'If at first you don't succeed, try, try again. Then use a stunt double.'*
>
> Arnold Schwarzenegger

Alternatively, you might conclude that you can't do something, but someone else can. There's nothing wrong with that, and Chapter 6 revealed scores of examples of people who strongly recommended complementing your own skills with those of outsiders and partners to make sure the job gets done.

That completes the setting up of your business tripwires, and possibly the detonation of some grenades. If you want to go into a lot more detail about how to get things done, look at my other book *Tick Achieve*. Now that you have worked out precisely what you want from your business, in the next chapter we will move on to identifying what you want from your personal life.

## Remember this: Effort v Result

Only put the effort in where it gets you somewhere. Think carefully before you rush into something. What effect will your action have? Is that what you want? Is it worth doing? It only takes a few seconds to work these things out.

## Focus points

✳ How have you arranged to trip yourself up?

✳ Over what time period?

✳ Have you put it in your personal organizer?

✳ Have you written it all down?

✳ What sanctions have you imposed on yourself?

✳ Have you resolved your idea, personal and business tripwires?

✳ Have you detonated your idea, personal and business grenades?

✳ Have you remembered to replace the spare, not the original?

✳ Are you a multitasker or a Rapid Sequential Tasker?

✳ Are you flogging any dead horses?

# 18

# Writing your Lifesmile Statement

In this chapter you will learn:

- ▶ *How to work out what you are like*
- ▶ *How to decide your own style*
- ▶ *How to decide what you really want*
- ▶ *How to write your own Lifesmile Statement*
- ▶ *How to have a board meeting with yourself*

As I mentioned earlier, there is no point in 'fixing' the business when you are not content yourself. So now we are going to force you to bare your soul (don't worry, you can do it in private if you want) so that you can accurately reconcile your working life with your personal wishes and aspirations. The process has five parts – four sets of questions you need to answer, and a concluding summary. So let's start.

# Part I: What am I like?

This is an exercise that I have often run in training sessions. Take a sheet of paper and write the question What am I like? at the top. Take ten minutes or so to write down your thoughts. This is supposed to be an honest assessment of how you come across. You can produce a series of notes, or a flow of observations, so long as it is what you genuinely think you are like. If relevant, you can highlight distinctions between how you think you come across, and how you really feel. If you have trouble doing this, try these questions.

▶ If someone met you for the first time, how would they describe you?

▶ How would you describe yourself to someone you have never met?

▶ Are there differences between your work and outside personality?

▶ Is your inner self significantly different from your outward persona?

**Unlock the facts:** What am I like?

This is potentially a scary exercise, but very revealing. Many people have never answered this question of themselves before. Take your time and be brutally honest. This will reveal what you might want to change.

# Part II: Decide your own style

The previous exercise will have weeded out whether you are being unrealistic about yourself or not. If you have never thought about it before, you now have a description of yourself to consider. There may be elements of your style in it, or maybe not. If there aren't, or if you want to change how you come across, the next step is to define that style. Take another ten minutes to answer these questions.

▶ Who or what is your favourite person or team(s)?

▶ What qualities make them so good?

▶ How can those qualities inspire your approach?

▶ Now define your own personal style.

So now you have a personal assessment and a defined style in front of you. Put that aside for a moment. We will come back to it in a minute.

**Try it now: What's your style?**

Everybody has a style, but you may never have paused to consider what it is. Now is the time to do it. Your personal style should dovetail perfectly with that of your business. If not, you may wish to adjust one or the other.

# Part III: So what do I *really* want?

So now we know what you are like, and what style you would like to emulate. Now let's get to the heart of what is going to make you happy in life. Answer these rather direct and personal questions on a separate sheet of paper.

▶ What's the point of my life?

▶ Why do I bother working?

▶ What, ultimately, do I want for myself?

▶ By when?

This needs to be a very honest exercise. There is no point in deluding yourself because you are the potential beneficiary, or loser, depending on how you reply. Your orientation should be 'I do this because ...'.

**Remember this:** What do you *really* want?

Your business should be a conduit for your personal aspirations. You can't reconcile the two unless you know what you really want. So make sure you know, and then you can do something about it.

# Part IV: I pledge ...

Take another blank piece of paper and write at the top of it 'I pledge'. Now write down what you are going to do differently from now on in order to achieve what you want. If you can't articulate it in your own words, answer these three questions.

▶ How exactly am I going to get where I want to be?

▶ Do I need help and, if so, from whom?

▶ By when will I achieve this?

**Try it now:** Your pledge

Try writing down your pledge. This could be to yourself, your business, your family or friends. Writing something down and pinning it on the wall has a polarizing effect. Live with your pledge and see if you can live up to it.

# Part V: My Lifesmile Statement

You have now effectively written all the elements of your Lifesmile Statement. It should have four parts so far, and we will now complete it with a fifth – the summary. Collect the four pieces of paper you should now have, and put them together. If you prefer, type them all out on one sheet along the lines shown below.

1  This is what I am like

2  This is my personal style

3  What I really want is

4  I pledge ...

All you have to do now is answer one final question.

5  If there's one thing I am going to do it is ...

This completes your Lifesmile Statement. Everything on it is designed to make you happy, and if you manage to do what it says, you certainly will be. So print it out, blow it up large and stick it on the wall to remind yourself every day what you are all about.

This is what I am like:

_____

This is my personal style:

_____

What I really want is:

_____

I pledge:

_____

If there's one thing I am going to do it is:

_____

My Lifesmile Statement.

### Remember this: My Lifesmile Statement

Consolidate all the elements of your thinking into one statement: what you are like, your style, what you want, and what you pledge. This is a powerful statement of intent that should serve both your personal and business lives well.

**Part I: What am I like?**

- If someone met you for the first time, how would they describe you?
- How would you describe yourself to someone you have never met?
- Are there differences between your work and outside personality?
- Is your inner self significantly different from your outward persona?

**Part II: Decide your own style**

- Who or what is your favourite person or team(s)?
- What qualities make them so good?
- How can those qualities inspire your approach?
- Now define your own personal style

**Part III: What do I *really* want?**

- What's the point of my life?
- Why do I bother working?
- What, ultimately, do I want for myself?
- By when?

**Part IV: I pledge ...**

- How exactly am I going to get where I want to be?
- Do I need help and, if so, from whom?
- By when will I achieve this?

**Part V: My Lifesmile Statement**

- If there's one thing I am going to do it is:

**Figure 18.1** Complete Lifesmile Statement method.

# Try being angular

There are lots of ways to answer the questions we have just posed. If the answers come naturally to you, then move on to the next chapter or take a breather. These personal matters can be a bit harrowing sometimes. But if you developed writer's block, here are some suggestions to drag your answers out of you. They are in there somewhere. You can try the same method that we used to determine the future of the business, by simply stating your one-year, three-year, five-year or ten-year aims for yourself. If not, be a bit more perverse. See if you agree or disagree with these assertions.

► To stay interesting, you have to stay angry.

► A happy owner means a good business.

► It is good to be conventionally odd.

► Big picture, small picture, forget the picture – it doesn't matter.

► Never apologize, never explain.

If you agree, write down why, and how you personally enact that approach. If you disagree, write down why, plus your alternative.

> *'I'm always doing things I can't do. That's how I get to do them.'*
>
> Pablo Picasso

Push yourself to have aspirations that are beyond what you currently do. It keeps you stimulated and increases your chances of success when you are growing your business, because interested students are more tenacious about their subject. In short, consider doing some things you have never done.

# A board meeting with yourself

Another way of dealing with writer's block is to imagine having a board meeting with yourself. Of course, self-employed people do this all the time, and they are very used to mulling over conflicting thoughts on their own. It is a technique you can use when you have lots of colleagues too. Imagine that you are in a board meeting, and that you are being subjected to intense questioning. Take the nastiest questions that you didn't fancy answering from the process in this chapter, and pretend that you absolutely have to answer. If you still can't produce anything, ask a partner, close friend, or someone who knows nothing about your business, to force you to answer them.

> *'A fanatic is one who can't change his mind and won't change the subject.'*
>
> Winston Churchill

## Nailing a jelly to the wall

An exasperated colleague of mine once exclaimed: 'I'm trying to nail a jelly to the wall here'. Bear in mind that if something is vague, it's useless, so you must have clear statements about what you desire for your future. Keep it clear and keep it fresh.

> *'When you've run out of red, use blue!'*
>
> Pablo Picasso

### Focus points

* Have you clarified what you are like?
* Have you decided your own style?
* Have you written down what you really want?
* Have you made some pledges?
* If so, what are they?
* Have you completed your Lifesmile Statement?
* Have you tried some new angles?
* Are you able to have a board meeting with yourself?
* Is your plan clear and fresh?
* Are you ready to pin it on the wall?

# 19

## Don't confuse movement with progress

In this chapter you will learn:

▶ *How not to confuse movement with progress*

▶ *How to concentrate on action, not activity*

▶ *How to concentrate on outcome, not output*

▶ *How to identify and avoid obfuscation*

▶ *That business does not have to mean being busy*

Much ado about nothing. Lots of movement but no forward motion. All talk and no action. How many times have you observed in life that a lot appears to be happening, but in fact, nothing much really is? That is what this chapter is all about. If you run a business, or wish to grow one successfully, then you haven't got the time, nor probably the patience, to allow people to faff about, or events to drift along, when what they are doing has no particular bearing on the main point. It is what the Italians call the English Disease: rushing around creating the *impression* that things are happening, but with no real tangible results.

Before I continue, I need to acknowledge the inspiration behind the chapter's title. My brother has a friend who is an experienced diplomat. They were driving on the motorway one day when an overtaking car sped rapidly into a gap just in front of them. The diplomat, an experienced pilot as well as a highly competent driver, declared: 'Don't confuse movement with progress.' The moral lies in an ability to move towards the intended objective without undue histrionics which, although they create the impression of activity, have no true bearing on the ultimate outcome. This is a vital lesson for anyone in business. Let's have a look at some other ways of phrasing it.

▶ Commando raids are good. Carpet bombing isn't.

▶ Laser strikes are good. Detonating everything isn't.

▶ Specific things are good. Generating lots of stuff to do isn't.

▶ Orderly progress to an intended destination is good. Buzzing around like a fly in a bottle isn't.

▶ It is better to arrive quietly than to make a big noise trying to get there.

This last one sounds like an ancient Chinese proverb, but it isn't. I just made it up. But you get the idea. Do not allow yourself to be fooled by a smokescreen of activity when you know very well it is simply to disguise the fact that the main item is not being done.

# Action not activity

A lot of modern business people think that they are really clever if they are busy. I disagree. The smart operator knows how to have things working for them. What's so clever about being busy? All you need is a certain amount of activity to keep you stimulated, leaving the remainder of the time for you to pursue the things that really matter to you. Any fool can appear to be permanently busy. If you ring someone for an appointment and they can offer you a 'window of opportunity' in six months' time, then there are two possible explanations. The first is that they are hugely in demand, and thoroughly enjoying every second of it. In which case, good luck to them. The second (more likely) reason is that they are not in control of their own life and have too many meetings discussing stuff that doesn't have much bearing on the main point. Which applies to you?

From the training sessions I have run over the past few years, I have learnt that the average amount of time that people in service industries spend bogged down in meetings is between 40 and 80 per cent of their working week. This figure is staggering. When you consider that the majority of meetings are to discuss how to move something forward, this statistic begs the question of when exactly these people are supposed to find the time to enact all the things that are raised in these apparently highly important meetings. If you want something to happen, concentrate on the action, not on activity that makes it look as though action is occurring.

### Unlock the facts: Action not activity

Some people love to look busy, but often what they are doing has no bearing on the matter in hand. Concentrate on sensible action rather than generating activity for the sake of it.

# Outcome not output

Meetings are not the only culprit in this context. In many corporations, bureaucracy is endemic. So often they make it look as though something is happening, when frequently it isn't.

The output of an organization really doesn't matter much. It is the outcome that matters. If you achieve something excellent, who cares how you got there? If you have a great idea, who cares whether it happened in a flash, or over two weeks, or several years? Can you imagine someone saying: *'What a great idea. I wonder how many meetings they needed to make that happen?'* I don't think so. Here is a list of business activities that, more often than not, are a waste of time.

► Meetings

► Conference calls

► Status reports

► Reports

► Travelling

► Communal emails

I can hear you exclaiming now. 'He is completely wrong! We couldn't function without these things!' But look again, and you will see that I have said 'more often than not'. This is the point. With some careful thought and application, you should be able to reduce your output by half, so that you can concentrate on the outcome. Try asking yourself some of these questions.

► Do I really need to have that meeting?

► Does it need to be that long?

► Do all those people need to be there?

► Do I need this piece of paperwork?

► Does anyone else?

► Does that need to be written down?

► Do I need to send that email?

► Do I need to have that conversation?

► Does that even need to be discussed?

There are hundreds of questions that can change your working life. In Chapter 15, we looked at Lee Iacocca saying: 'They tell me what they think. Then I decide.' If you are good at business, you weigh up the situation, make a decision, and then get on with it. It can save hours, days, even years of hanging about. So the best question of all is:

▶ Can we just get on with it?

This question will blow the doors off most government departments and have millions of big corporate citizens dashing to their subsidized canteens for a cheap cappuccino. For many more questions like this, read my other book *So What?* You see, most people *want* to look busy, regardless of whether there is an outcome. Don't let that person be you.

### Remember this: Outcome not output

Generating huge amounts of stuff (output) may have nothing to do with the end result (outcome). So before you produce endless documents and spreadsheets, work out your desired outcome and work backwards from there.

## Spotting obfuscation

There will be plenty reading this who will think that the author has gone a bit barmy at this point, but bear with me. Have you ever heard of obfuscation?

**Obfuscation** (*noun*): the act or an instance of making something deliberately obscure or difficult to understand

It's not quite the same as time wasting. It is nothing to do with being idle or unintelligent. No, it is much smarter than that. It is about making something appear more complicated than it truly is, or needs to be. Lots of professions do it all the time. People have to hire lawyers because they have surrounded themselves with a language that no one else can understand. City traders are the same. Most industries have a jargon that provides a force field which is designed to exclude everyone else. That enables them to appear clever, and to cast a veil over their activities. That in turn allows them to charge more for their services and generally feel superior. All industries do it. It isn't even a particularly evil activity. It seems to happen naturally. You know the kind of thing.

> *'Jane was talking to Dave about the ZXC. Of course, he said it was ludicrous that the project manager never filled in the 87-K, and now that LOD have got hold of it, it'll probably be sent to the pit bulls in back-end architecture or thrown into the hands of AWOB with the rest of the ideas from Project Azalea.'*

Impenetrable rubbish, I am sure you will agree. Under no circumstances should you ever end up talking like this. It undermines your credibility and makes you sound less intelligent than you are. If you remain unconvinced that there is too much language in business that encourages confusion, have a look at the range of phrases in use to describe unnecessary talk.

**blather** (Scottish: blether): foolish talk; nonsense

**drivel:** unintelligible language

**hot air:** empty talk

**jabber:** to speak without making sense

**nonsense:** something that makes no sense

**piffle:** nonsense

**rabbit:** to talk inconsequentially

**static:** interference in transmissions

**verbiage:** excessive and often meaningless use of words

**waffle:** to speak in a vague and wordy manner

**whim-wham:** something fanciful; a trifle

**white noise:** sound with wide continuous range of frequencies of uniform intensity

I have barely scratched the surface. The list goes on and on, and the descriptive vocabulary for this phenomenon is so rich precisely *because* it is such a frequent occurrence. But be under no illusion: if you want to get something done, you haven't got time for this sort of prevarication. Life is not that complicated, and business certainly doesn't have to be.

> *'There cannot be a crisis next week. My schedule is already full.'*
>
> Henry Kissinger

You will have heard the axiom that work expands to fit the time available in which to do it. The alternative, of course, is that you are too busy to create the time for anything else. Neither extreme makes any sense. Why surround yourself with irrelevant things to do, when you have lots of other genuinely interesting things to do? Something of a rhetorical question perhaps, but we all have examples of circumstances in which nothing important is getting done because too much irrelevant stuff is being done instead. If you suspect that this might be the case with your business, or with any of your customers, then you have some serious thinking to do.

**Unlock the facts:** Spotting obfuscation

Are you making something more complicated than it needs to be? If so, stop it. If one of your staff is, then give them permission to make it simpler. If a customer is, then offer to simplify it. Really, there is no reason ever for obfuscation.

# Business does not mean being busy

Busy used to mean (literally) being actively or fully engaged, and there's nothing wrong with that. But it has also come to mean overcrowded with detail, and that is not a good thing. Never confuse movement with progress. Work out the bits that matter, and do them only. If you have spare time, do something you want to do in order to ensure your sustained happiness, not something that supports the idea that you are frantically busy. Try these phrases to puncture the idea that being busy is beneficial.

▶ Claiming to be too busy is the last refuge of an ailing businessperson.

- Being busy used to be macho – now it is gender neutral.
- If you are too busy, you have no time for yourself.
- If you are too busy, you have no time for anyone else.
- If you are too busy, you are one-dimensional.
- If you are too busy, you are missing the point.
- If you are too busy, you are missing out on life.
- If you are too busy, you are incompetent.

**Remember this: Business or busyness?**

Businesses don't actually have to be busy. A certain amount of work, judiciously undertaken for the right price, could liberate weeks of free time. So before you make yourself perpetually busy, consider what the business can do for you.

# There's a tidal wave coming. Here's a paper cup

Many people in business feel that they are under-equipped to deal with what life is going to throw at them. They feel as though they have been given a paper cup, and told that there is a tidal wave coming. But coping with business, or 'busyness', is all about guessing the landscape and the possible outcomes before they occur. This is not nearly as difficult as you might think. The first step is to realize that things may well go wrong before they go wrong. That's not a particularly complicated idea now is it? Put even more simply, assume the worst, and do your best. Life's a mess. Adapt. Be prepared for changes and make it up as you go along. Plan B is often better than Plan A. Stick to the simple stuff, and don't let administration and bureaucracy get in the way. If you view business as a nasty tidal wave, then your perspective needs some adjustment. Try asking yourself these questions.

- What is likely to happen?
- When?

- What can I do to anticipate that?
- What can I do to prepare for that?
- What can I do to influence that?
- What can I do to prevent that?
- What can I do to make that tolerable?

It is a form of disaster planning, except that these are not disasters. They are just the normal nuisances that happen in business every day.

> 'A change of nuisances is as good as a holiday.'
>
> David Lloyd George

**Try it now: Most things are predictable**

You don't have to be Nostradamus to predict most things that will happen to your business in the next week, month or year. So work out what those things are and make plans so that you are not caught by surprise.

# Everything busier than everything else

Don't confuse movement with progress. The illusion that things will be better when they are busier needs careful consideration, because it doesn't make any sense. Do you really agree with the idea that if there is a lot happening, then progress is being made? The old joke goes that when marketing activity does not have the desired effect, Marketing Directors immediately do more of it. Instead, they would be better placed to work out why it didn't work first, and then make their next move. What do politicians do when they see light at the end of the tunnel? Order more tunnel! So before you rush around like a headless chicken without knowing why, ask yourself these questions.

- Why am I doing this?
- What's wrong with things as they are?
- Will the proposed activity get me anywhere?

- Is this worth doing?
- Why?
- What is the likely return in relation to my efforts?
- Is this the beginning, the middle or the end of the sequence?
- Do I need to rethink this?

At the heart of all this is the maxim: 'Never do anything unless you know why you are doing it.' No one is proposing that you become idle – simply that you do not fool yourself into believing that all the rushing around you are doing is achieving anything, unless of course you have genuinely worked out that it definitely is. In which case, move on to the next chapter immediately.

## Focus points

- Have you confused movement with progress?
- Have you banished activity in favour of action?
- Can you spot obfuscation?
- If so, what have you done to eradicate it?
- Have you reduced the amount of bureaucracy in your life?
- Have you asked why you can't just get on with it?
- Do you often claim to be too busy?
- Is it really true?
- Have you anticipated what is likely to happen before it does?
- Ask again: why am I doing this?

# 20

# Everything may or may not be related to everything else

In this chapter you will learn:

▶ *That everything may or may not be related to everything else*

▶ *How to thrive on chaos*

▶ *How action can lead to chain reaction*

▶ *That everything changes all the time*

▶ *To ask yourself regularly whether you have actually done it*

So now we will finish off with a light-hearted look at how everything may or may not be related to everything else.

## 'Butterfly destroys city': chaos theory revisited

Everything may or may not be related to everything else. Cause and effect is a well-established concept. In one extreme example, a butterfly landing on a tree in a rainforest in South America leads to a chain of events that sees a city destroyed by a hurricane thousands of miles away. At a more personal level, if I do x, then y will probably happen. It all makes perfect sense. And yet, people believe just as much in chance, superstition, fate, and a whole range of other ideas that are essentially random. So *can* you predict what is going to happen to you or your business? Or does it all just occur anyway?

> **Chaos theory** (*noun*): a theory, applied in various branches of science, that apparently random phenomena have underlying order

Now there's a heavy concept. Chaos theory is suggesting that, even though everything looks as though it is happening randomly, it actually has some sort of order. This is not a philosophy book, so I don't think we need to spend time diligently presenting the pros and cons, but it certainly is a big idea. So does that mean that everything in your business is related to everything else? Well, it might do, but then again it might not.

**Remember this:** Chaos theory

Be aware that small changes in one part of your business could affect things elsewhere. Think this through before you act. Equally, keep an eye open for subtle changes in your customers. This may provide early warning of bigger changes to come.

# Action and chain reaction

Most actions lead to a reaction, and if pushed to the furthest degree, that could become a chain reaction. The question is whether this matters or not. Well, it might matter on three counts.

1 You want something to happen as a result of your actions.

2 You do not want something to happen as a result of your actions.

3 You don't know what will happen as a result of your actions.

It all boils down to:

> If I do x, they will do y. Do I want this to happen?

If you are in position number one, then go ahead and do whatever you want to do. If it is number two, then you need to think hard about whether you really do want to do it, or what contingency plans you have in mind. If it is scenario three, then you probably haven't thought about it enough, so pause and think.

> *'Very few things happen at the right time, and the rest do not happen at all. The conscientious historian will correct these defects.'*
>
> Herodotus

If you are not much of a fan of the cause and effect principle, you nevertheless have to cope with stuff happening. The sequence in which it happens is immaterial – how are you going to deal with it all? As Herodotus points out, very few things happen at the right time. The more experienced people become when running businesses, the more they conclude that very few things have a predictable pattern. Just when you think they do, they don't. That means that you usually have to make it up as you go along. He also points out that most things do not happen at 'the right time'. Suffice to say, you cannot plan a business on supposition, and some would say that you can barely plan at all.

**Try it now:** Action and chain reaction

If you take action, it's not that difficult to predict the possible reaction, or even a chain reaction that may follow. Consider this before you act. It could save a lot of aggravation caused by thoughtless, hasty action.

# Everything changes

I was once taking a short break in Ireland, and I wandered into a newsagent to buy a paper. As I walked out of the door, the owner called after me, 'Come back tomorrow, there'll be more news then.'

The remark has always stuck with me. Apart from being very funny, it is also highly perspicacious when it comes to the recurring nature of news or events. There is always more news. That applies to businesses just as much as every other aspect of life. So, assume there will be more news to deal with, and roll with it. There is great merit in planning, as many parts of this book advocate, but you have to be flexible. Here is a rough sequence that the flexible businessperson should follow.

► Plan it

► Do it

► Change it

► Do it differently.

This applies equally to your own subject matter as it does to the manner in which you might wish to react to competitive manoeuvres. Zig when they zag is a common strategy for constantly staying distinctive in relation to your competitors. In the new ultra-flexible world, this could be updated to zig when they zag, and then zog.

**Remember this:** Everything changes

Do not become set in your ways. Things change all the time. Get used to the idea and adapt frequently. Sometimes it may even be in your interests to change before your customers do.

# It's all in your mind

*'Half this game is 90 per cent mental.'*
Philadelphia Phillies manager Danny Ozark

Of course we have all had some fun at the expense of sports managers and commentators for the way they trip over their words. And yet there is always a truism lurking beneath the gobbledegook. Much of it is to do with aspects of psychology, and many phrases are transferable to a business context. For example, many coaches refuse to discuss the opposition because they are not interested in adapting their way of playing to allow for their opponents' system. They want it to happen the other way round. 'Never discuss the competition' is an interesting maxim, and there are even examples of 'uncompetitive reviews', where the business is reviewed but the competition is not allowed to be discussed for fear of diluting exciting ideas with too much knowledge. Here is another essential weapon in your mental armoury.

▶ Do I value their opinion?

It is a very powerful question. If someone says something that disturbs you, or with which you do not agree, ask yourself whether you value their opinion. If not, move on and don't lose sleep over it. Only pay attention to observations from a source that you intrinsically respect. Your confidence and happiness are all relative, and they are all in the mind.

## Unlock the facts: All in the mind

Self-confidence is utterly crucial when you run your own business. Work hard at building and retaining your self-esteem. If you are wobbling, seek help from trusted friends and advisers. You can't fix your business if you haven't fixed yourself.

# Yes, but have you actually done it?

There are all sorts of ideas in this book, and hopefully they will have triggered many more. But none of them are any use to you unless you actually do some of them. So, if you have been drifting through this book and thinking, 'That's a good idea', then now is the time to get on with it. An idea is only as good as its implementation.

**Unlock the facts:** Have you done it?

Do not let yourself get away with being slapdash. Half-finished ideas, products and services are no use to anyone. Embark on a manageable number of things and get them done.

# Closing remarks

> *'How can I conclude until I hear what I have to say?'*
>
> Anonymous

My father was once sitting in a formal Air Force presentation at which a senior dignitary was droning on. Someone at the back, risking a court martial or some other heinous punishment, muttered, 'Come to the point.' Against all the odds, the speaker heard the remark, looked up from behind his half-moon spectacles, and responded to the heckler: 'How can I conclude until I hear what I have to say?' A brilliant riposte for sure, and a moral lies within. Make sure you take the time to hear yourself out. That has been the theme of this book. Business survival is all about careful thought. Give yourself the thinking time that you deserve and need in order to achieve a decent result.

> *'Somebody's boring me. I think it's me.'*
>
> Dylan Thomas

Equally, don't drag it out for ages. Some careful thought is good. Paralysis by analysis is not. Get the conditions right. Consider the wider context. Pick and choose the bits that work for you, but don't be slavish about it. Try some structured thinking. Whittle it down to the elements that you think are going to help. Make sure you keep your personal interests firmly at the centre of it. Don't get distracted or knocked off course by extraneous factors. Just get on and do it. That's it. Now, before I outstay my welcome, I am going to stop. Off you go then, and good luck.

*'Nothing is my last word on anything.'*

Henry James

## Focus points

* What do you think: are things related?
* If so, can you determine cause and effect?
* If not, how are you going to deal with random events?
* Have you got your head straight?
* Have you set aside some decent thinking time?
* Have you applied some interesting techniques?
* What did your thinking reveal?
* Have you actually done what you decided to?
* Have you considered yourself in all of this?
* Do you feel reinvigorated?

# Taking it further

Adair, John, *The Art of Creative Thinking* (Kogan Page, 2007)

Allen, David, *Getting Things Done* (Piatkus, 2001)

Ashton, Robert, *Achieving Business Alchemy* (Hodder & Stoughton, 2002)

—*The Entrepreneur's Book of Checklists* (Pearson, 2004)

—*The Life Plan* (Pearson, 2007)

Benson, Nigel, *Introducing Psychology* (Icon, 2004)

Branson, Richard, *Screw it, let's do it* (Virgin, 2006)

Duncan, Kevin, *So What?* (Capstone, 2007)

—*Start* (Capstone, 2008)

—*Tick Achieve* (Capstone, 2009)

—*Small Business Survival* (Hodder, 2010)

—*Run Your Own Business* (Hodder, 2010)

—*What You Need To Know About Starting A Business* (Capstone, 2011)

—*The Diagrams Book* (LID 2013)

—*The Ideas Book* (LID 2014)

—*The Smart Thinking Book* (LID 2015)

Earls, Mark, *Herd* (John Wiley, 2007)

Gerber, Michael E., *The E Myth Revisited* (Harper Collins, 1995)

Gladwell, Malcolm, *Blink* (Allen Lane, 2005)

—*Outliers* (Little Brown, 2008)

—*The Tipping Point* (Little Brown, 2000)

Hodgkinson, Tom, *How To Be Idle* (Penguin, 2004)

Maeda, John, *The Laws Of Simplicity* (MIT Press, 2006)

Maier, Corinne, *Hello Laziness* (Orion, 2005)

Milligan and Smith, *See Feel Think Do* (Marshall Cavendish, 2006)

Morgan, Adam, *The Pirate Inside* (John Wiley, 2004)

O'Connell, Fergus, *Simply Brilliant* (Prentice Hall, 2001)

Pagan, Michael *Managing IT for Small Businesses* (Hodder & Stoughton, 2007)

Quinn, Robert E., *Moments of Greatness* (Harvard Business Review, 2005)

Semler, Ricardo, *The Seven-Day Weekend* (Century, 2003)

Tupman, Simon, *Why Entrepreneurs Should Eat Bananas* (Cyan, 2006)

# Index